IROQUOIS JOURNEY

**The Iroquoians and
Their World**

EDITORS

José António Brandão
Mary Druke Becker
William A. Starna

IROQUOIS JOURNEY

AN ANTHROPOLOGIST REMEMBERS

William N. Fenton

Edited and introduced by
Jack Campisi
and
William A. Starna

University of Nebraska Press
Lincoln & London

All photographs from the author's collection,
courtesy Iroquois Indian Museum, Howes Cave, New York.

Manufactured in the United States of America

⊗

Library of Congress Cataloging-in-Publication Data
Fenton, William Nelson, 1908–2005
Iroquois journey: an anthropologist remembers / William
N. Fenton; edited and introduced by Jack Campisi and
William A. Starna.
p. cm. — (The Iroquoians and their world)
Includes bibliographical references and index.
ISBN-13: 978-0-8032-2021-8 (cloth: alk. paper)
ISBN-10: 0-8032-2021-9 (cloth: alk. paper)
ISBN-13: 978-0-8032-2789-7 (paper: alk. paper)
1. Fenton, William Nelson, 1908–2005 2. Indianists—New
York (State)—Biography. 3. Anthropologists—New York
(State)—Biography. 4. Iroquoian Indians—New York
(State)—Antiquities. 5. New York (State)—Antiquities.
I. Campisi, Jack. II. Starna, William A. III. Title.
E76.45.F46F46 2007
301.092—dc22
[B]
2007009527

Set in ITC New Baskerville.

CONTENTS

PHOTOS

Jack Campisi and William A. Starna

A scholar's lifework is measured not only by what of lasting value was accomplished but also by how things were done, and to what end. A case in point is the extraordinary career of anthropologist William Nelson Fenton, who for more than seven decades dedicated himself to understanding, objectifying, and making plain the culture history of an American Indian people: the Iroquois. That he succeeded in this enterprise is beyond question. In the process, Bill left us with a body of literature unmatched in Iroquoian studies, all bearing his distinctive intellectual mark. At the same time, he welcomed and encouraged the diversity of approaches that have come to characterize the field. His overriding concern was with the way Indian history was written—that what was presented reflected something of the "why" behind the actions of native people in their encounter with Euro-Americans. How Bill came to study the Iroquois, and the path he took in pursuit of their history, is a story worth knowing.

Introduced to anthropology in his last year at Dartmouth College, Bill in 1931 went on to graduate school at Yale University. There he was tutored by several of the field's most eminent practitioners: Edward Sapir, George Peter Murdock, Clark Wissler, and Leslie

Spier. His education took place during a period of significant growth and change in the discipline. Rejecting the unilineal, progressivist evolutionary theory of Lewis Henry Morgan—who incidentally had been among the first to systematically study the Iroquois—Bill's teachers had made the shift to historicism, specifically to the historical particularism of Franz Boas, the acknowledged "father" of modern American anthropology. In fact, all but Murdock had earned their doctorates with Boas at Columbia University.

The theoretical orientation of the Boasian school is characterized in the main by the collection and organization of ethnographic data derived almost exclusively from extensive, firsthand field work. Among North Americanists, including those who were drawn to the Iroquois, the favored methodology combined ethnographic, historical, archaeological, and linguistic approaches to produce generalizations about culture and culture processes.

Although Bill became and remained a Boasian, his theoretical views were neither doctrinaire nor Procrustean. For him the appeal of a multidisciplinary approach lay in its utility for controlling and understanding the complex and wide-ranging data that his research on the Iroquois generated. Along the way he selected for use one or the other theory as required by the problem under study, his important work on factionalism in American Indian societies (1955) being but one example.[1] As Anthony F. C. Wallace has described it:

> Fenton's career also can serve as the epitome of a certain kind of professional life in anthropology. He is and has always been an Iroquoianist, allowing himself only so much time with other subjects (Taos, Klamath, Blackfoot, Maori) as to give some added perspective to his view of Iroquois. This single-minded devotion to one group, and the emphasis on ethnographic and historical description and classification (although always illumined by, and illuminating, theory) makes Fenton's role unique among American anthropologists of my acquaintance.[2]

Bill's ability to remain focused on Iroquoia is even more surprising given the uncertainty of a career in anthropology during the years of the Great Depression, the Second World War, and the immediate post-war period. His professional life began in 1935 as an employee of the United States Indian Service on the Tonawanda Reservation, near Akron, New York, while still completing his doctorate. After receiving his degree in 1937, Bill introduced and taught anthropology for a year and a half at St. Lawrence University in New York's north country. In 1939 he joined the Bureau of American Ethnology as ethnologist, serving with distinction in that post until 1951. There he was welcomed by the likes of anthropologists John R. Swanton, David I. Bushnell Jr., Henry B. Collins, John P. Harrington, and to a lesser extent, Aleš Hrdlička. From his office in the landmark "brownstone tower" of the Smithsonian Institution, he played an active role at the Smithsonian War Committee and the Ethnogeographic Board among other projects. Then, from 1952 to 1954, while a member of the National Research Council, he became the first to hold the position of executive secretary of the Division of Anthropology and Psychology. Beginning in 1954, and for the next thirteen years, Bill was assistant commissioner of the New York State Museum and Science Service, directing the state museum in Albany. There he initiated several major programmatic changes in the Science Service and oversaw the early planning for the new state museum and library, part of the ambitious South Mall project launched by Gov. Nelson Rockefeller, who had been a classmate of Bill's at Dartmouth. In 1968 Bill returned to university teaching as a member of the faculty of the State University of New York at Albany, retiring as Distinguished Professor of Anthropology in June 1979. But things did not end there. Bill continued to write and publish and to inspire others to do the same, now in the role as "Dean of Iroquois Studies."

Bill not only contemplated, undertook, and completed a rigorous and far-reaching program of research on the Iroquois but actively engaged a host of students and colleagues to follow his lead. Fred Voget, ethnologist and long time Fenton associate, has written that Bill left his mark on the field in many ways.[3] Early in his career, he prepared a series of "position papers" intended to keep scholars up-to-date on the state of Iroquois research and to direct them to matters that required attention ("Problems Arising," 1940; "Iroquois Studies," 1951), a number of which still wait to be addressed. Bill introduced the method of analysis referred to as "historical upstreaming," which he has described as "reading history backwards." This approach became an integral part of the discipline and methodology of ethnohistory—the application of the critical apparatus of ethnology to history—of which Bill is considered a founder.[4] Anthropologist Thomas Abler properly notes that:

> As one of ethnohistory's pioneers, Bill Fenton played a leading role in its legitimation as a scholarly endeavor. The number of scholars who identify themselves as ethnohistorians or as students of Indian history, and the quantity of work they produce, has multiplied enormously since Fenton published his paper on Iroquois suicide in 1941, since he addressed the American Anthropological Association on the training of historical ethnologists in America in 1951, and since he stood before the American Indian Ethnohistoric Conference (now the American Society for Ethnohistory) as the organization's incoming president in 1961.[5]

Ethnohistorians continue to produce the most informed writings on the interwoven histories of native peoples and Euro-Americans.

To advance the study of Iroquois culture history, Bill annually drew together students and scholars for the Conference on Iroquois Research, which he founded with Merle Deardorff and Charles Congdon at Red House on the Allegany Reservation in western New York in 1945. Today this unique gathering, which recently celebrated its sixtieth anniversary and whose participants represent all of the disciplines that have been brought to bear on the study of the Iroquois, meets at the Rensselaerville Institute, an hour's drive from Albany. Informal papers are the norm, followed by constructive give and take on the issues at hand. It is in this collegial atmosphere of common purpose where ideas are nurtured and tested.

Bill likewise organized efforts to tackle key problems in Iroquois studies such as, for example, exploring the localized character of Iroquois culture and communities and the relationship between Cherokee and Iroquois cultures ("Locality," 1951; *Symposium*, 1961). In a number of articles and presentations, he informed colleagues and students about the wealth of historical and ethnographic materials to be studied that would shed light on culture change, and he compiled and made available source lists and bibliographies for future reference. Of particular note in this regard is his influential *American Indian and White Relations to 1830: Needs and Opportunities for Study* (1957).

Bill long encouraged and supported research in linguistics and archaeology as a means by which to fill out the record of Iroquois history. His interests in these subfields of anthropology followed from a seminar on phonetics he took with Sapir while at Yale, his own fieldwork on the Seneca language, his long friendship with Floyd Lounsbury, as well as an early if brief experience on a dig along the Missouri. This abiding concern with interdisciplinary approaches fit perfectly Bill's Boasian world view, and it was the cornerstone upon which he built his career and guided the Conference on Iroquois Research.

Voget's appraisal of thirty years ago, when Bill was well into midstride, brings us to the question of the outcome of his research initiatives. It is one that is easily answered. There is not a single student of the Iroquois, areas of interest and expertise aside, who does not owe a considerable intellectual debt to Bill Fenton. Moreover, as if to lead by example, Bill continued to produce standard-setting works that reflected research goals he had identified early on. The most notable of these include Father J. F. Lafitau's *Customs of the American Indians* begun with Elizabeth Moore in 1939 (1974, 1977); *The False Faces of the Iroquois* (1987); *The Great Tree and the Longhouse: A Political History of the Iroquois Confederacy* (1998); and, what will surely stand as a paragon of ethnography, *The Little Water Medicine Society of the Senecas* (2002).

On a bright October day in 2003, colleagues, friends, and family converged on Cooperstown, at the foot of picturesque Otsego Lake in upstate New York, to celebrate the life and career of Bill Fenton. He would soon turn ninety-five.[6] This was not the first time that such a gathering had taken place, and like the others, it brought together many of the same people. We remember Bill's investiture as Distinguished Professor, University at Albany, in 1979, when Anthony F. C. Wallace delivered the honorary lecture in a room filled with familiar faces. Three years later, at the annual Conference on Iroquois Research, Bill was unanimously proclaimed "Dean of Iroquoian Studies." A festschrift, *Extending the Rafters,* soon followed. Bill was feted again by his fellows in 1995 on the fiftieth anniversary of that same conference, when for good measure he was presented with an award for perfect attendance. And then there was his ninetieth birthday party at his home in Slingerlands, New York, attended by folks from all over the map.

Bill was the recipient of numerous accolades over the course of a distinguished and productive career. A selection includes the Peter Doctor Award of the Seneca Nation (1958), the Cornplanter

Medal for Iroquois Research (1965), and the Distinguished Service Award of the American Anthropological Association (1983). In 1978 Bill was made Citizen Laureate of the University of Albany Foundation, and in 1999 he was awarded the prestigious Wilbur Lucius Cross Medal for Distinguished Alumni of the Yale Graduate School. But there is no similar instance we can think of that so well captured the substance of Bill's scholarly contributions and his influence on the field of anthropology and not incidentally, the substance of the man, as the occasion on that early fall day.

Central to the organizing principles of Iroquois communities is the emphasis placed on the obligations that obtain between members of the same generation and, equally important, between persons who are a generation or more apart. Together with other motifs and manifestations of reciprocity—the very essence of Iroquois society—these obligations give form to the bonds of continuity that, as Bill has written, "kept it in being." So it was with the community that had joined to honor Bill in Cooperstown.

As he had done nearly a quarter of a century earlier, Tony Wallace, half a generation younger than the man he referred to as mentor and friend, opened the program. Returning once again to the theme of "extending the rafters," he reflected on how well this metaphor for the acceptance of other native communities and refugees into the shelter of the Longhouse defined Bill's continued program of research and publication, not to mention his "constant recruitment and lifelong encouragement and inspiration of new students of Iroquois history and culture."

With Bill taking the lead, the "old people" were well represented. (This referent, we hasten to add, applies not only to chronological seniors, but more importantly, to intellectually valued statuses—in Bill's words, people "who know everything.") There was Tony of course and Harold Conklin, recently retired anthropologist, who spoke warmly about his and Bill's scholarly kinship and their common descent from Yale. As he finished his comments, Hal stepped from the rostrum and delivered a perfect rendering of *kanoieo: wi:ˀ*, a song announcing the "Feast of Dreams" at Midwinter, one that he had learned from listening to recordings Bill had made of Seneca singers in the 1930s. "I closed my eyes for a moment as if I were back in Coldspring," Bill told us.

Also stepping forward as a member of this age grade was Ernie Benedict, a Mohawk elder and activist from the native community of Akwesasne, which sits astride the border of the United States and Canada. Ernie had been Bill's student at St. Lawrence, just down the road, in 1937 and provided the gathering with reminiscences from those early days. Among the many accomplishments and contributions Ernie would make in service to his people and "the coming faces"—Mohawk youth—was the founding of the North American Indian Traveling College.

From the Mohawks—"keepers of the eastern door" of the confederacy—attention shifted to the Senecas, one of the "Three Brothers" of Longhouse Iroquois whose duty it was to watch over the "western door." Maxine Crouse Dowler, Bill recalled, was a teenager when as a graduate student and "novice fieldworker" he first pitched his tent "in Jonas Snow's dooryard." Maxine's parents, Clifford and Myrtie Crouse, had welcomed Bill into their home. A talented student, Maxine trained as a teacher, later became a mediator for Seneca children, and then a member of the local school board. In 2003 she was honored with the New York State Women of Distinction Award by the American Association of University Women and the New York State legislature. Today she is a leader in the Beaver Clan at Allegany, a position long held by her maternal grandmother. Maxine recounted for Bill the time, many years ago, when she spirited his son John away to dance with the Husk Faces on the sixth night of the Midwinter ceremonies at Coldspring.

Last among the "old people" was linguist Wallace Chafe, a student of Floyd Lounsbury, whose lineage also originated at Yale. It was Floyd who introduced Wally to Bill, then fully involved in the second trimester of his career as director of the New York State Museum. "I have always retained a vivid image of the three of us talking in Bill's office," Wally told us, "along with a couple of representatives of the Education Department who seemed woefully uninformed about the Iroquois, alleging that they had nothing that could be called a culture. The three of us were taken aback, Bill wondering afterward how he and Floyd could have built their careers on something that didn't exist." Just then, Wally reminded us, the disastrous Kinzua dam project was getting off the ground, which would work to so tragically alter the lives of the Allegany Senecas.[7]

First to speak for the "young people," those from the generations that followed Bill's, was Thomas Abler from the University of Waterloo. Discharging his obligations, Tom thanked Bill for helping him find the right path. He then made us mindful of the debt owed to Bill for his years of research, writing, teaching, and example. This was especially true for the role Bill's ethnographic fieldwork played in the development of ethnohistory, in the eyes of many his most important scholarly contribution. This was all the more remarkable, Tom observed, "in an era when historical investigations were disparaged by a large and vocal portion of the anthropological community," for at the time, the school of British social anthropology was dominated by Bronislaw Malinowski and A. R. Radcliffe-Brown, both of whom were hostile to history.

Other presentations from the "young people" followed, including ours. As Bill's first PhD (Campisi) and his first graduate assistant (Starna, by way of Dean Snow), we spoke of our experiences as Bill's students. One of us commented on how in his teaching Bill insisted that his charges become familiar with and control as much of the literature as possible and then apply an informed, rigorous methodology to the problem at hand. And there was recognition of Bill's generosity toward his graduate students, often "subcontracting" projects to them from his own vast storehouse of ethnographic and historic data, which often were turned into conference presentations, articles, dissertations, and now and again books. The other of us had firsthand experience with Bill in the field during a trip to the Six Nations Reserve in Canada in the early 1970s. Bill was working with Jimmy Skye on a translation and annotation of the Tekanawita epic.[8] Borrowing a technique from Floyd Lounsbury, he used two Uher reel-to-reel tape recorders, the first to play the text and the second to record the text being played along with the translations, comments, and the discussions that went on. What was so impressive was the knowledge Bill possessed, the copious notes he took, and the rapport that was so evident between him and Jimmy, at a time when anthropologists were unwelcome in Iroquois communities.

In assessing Bill's career and his enormous and altogether original body of work, it is easy to miss the essential ingredients that made it all possible: forty-plus years of fieldwork and seventy-plus years focused on writing on one culture, its social organization, ceremonies, beliefs, material culture, history, and component societies. This is a commitment difficult to match, and a contribution even more difficult to equal. And he enjoyed every minute of it.

Nyawenh, Bill.

IROQUOIS JOURNEY

ONE

Upstaters in Suburbia and at Home

My career as an Iroquoianist may have been foretold three generations before my birth. The Fentons of Conewango Valley in western New York and the family of Amos Snow of the Seneca Nation had kept up an association going back to the 1860s. The Fenton farm on Flat Iron Road lay halfway between the Cattaraugus and Allegany reservations of the Seneca Nation, and Seneca families "going to the other side," as they said, camped on the hemlock ridge at the back of the farm. One bitter winter morning, my father's father at chore time reported to his widowed mother that smoke was rising from the ridge. His mother suggested that he go see how the Indians were faring. He took an ax and went afoot, intending to split up some firewood he had felled. He found an Indian family encamped in a lean-to they had constructed of hemlock boughs: a man, an old woman, and a young woman with a newborn baby. They were shivering.

When my grandfather returned to the house at noon for dinner, he reported what he had seen to his mother, who insisted that he hitch the team to the pung, fill the bed with straw, throw in a buffalo robe, and go fetch that family to the warm farmhouse. By suppertime she had installed the Indian family in the hired girl's room off the kitchen. The Seneca family stayed for a week, until the weather permitted travel. When they departed, the old woman thanked my great-grandmother for shelter, sustenance, and hospitality, saying it was the first time they had been invited to sleep and eat in a white home. It was the Indian custom, she added, to bind a friendship with a present, whereupon she unfolded an old burden strap, an obvious heirloom. It was decorated with dyed deer hair and porcupine-quill embroidery worked in a geometric pattern and edged with seed beads. She handed it to my great-grandmother, Fanny Carr, widow of Captain William, the seafarer.

The Seneca hunter was Amos Snow, a stout, jovial fellow who became a lifelong friend of my grandfather: a companion on squirrel- and pigeon-shooting expeditions, a fellow trotting-horse fancier, as well as being good for sharing labor on the farm. On occasion Amos would show up with his young family. At some point he entrusted to my grandfather two old wooden False Faces that he produced from under the wagon seat.[1] My grandfather kept them in a round wooden cheese box (see Fenton, *False Faces*, 1987). Later, Amos left a string of purple wampum that commemorated some event long since forgotten. These items, however they came to us, comprised the nucleus of an ethnological collection that was kept in the attic in a special room known as the "Indian collection," where I was privileged to climb steep stairs of a rainy summer afternoon. When visitors, sometimes Indians, came to the farm, I was allowed to tag along and listen. Among the guests were Warren King Morehead from Andover Academy, on his way to the Ohio mounds; Arthur C. Parker, then the New York state archaeologist; and M. R. Harrington, then of the American Museum of Natural History. Their comments aroused my curiosity.

Both of my parents hailed from southwestern New York State. My father, John William Fenton (1876–1939), grew up on the family farm in Conewango Valley, Cattaraugus County. My mother, Anna Belle Nourse (1873–1949), spent her girlhood in Mayville, the county seat of adjacent Chautauqua County in the remote corner of the state and home of the Chautauqua Institution, which afforded cultural advantages in music and the arts. They met at Fredonia Normal School, ancestor of the present state college of that name, where they were trained to teach at the elementary level, and they both found employment in the New York City school system in 1901. Mother landed at PS 9 in a bluestocking district on Riverside Drive, where she would become principal.

Father taught the children of recent immigrants at PS 158 on the upper East Side and ingratiated himself with their parents, of whom some became dealers in antiques and art objects. Father's talent was in painting and drawing, which he improved by study at the Parson's school and the Arts Students League, ultimately becoming a recognized still-life painter and having his works hung in major New York shows sponsored by the National Academy of Design and the New York Watercolor Society, to which he was elected. Neither parent attained the academic degrees so essential for advancement in the New York City school system, something that was no doubt responsible later for their motivating their own children to earn advanced degrees.

Married in 1906, they found a home in New Rochelle, just twenty minutes from Broadway, where father could commute via the new Boston and Westchester Electric Railway to 180th Street, and then via the Third Avenue El to 96th Street, close to PS 158. My sister, Frances, was born the next year. I followed at mid-December 1908, and my brother, Robert Bruce, another six years later. Each of us was delivered at home by our family physician, a florid-faced Irishman named Brennan, who always gave an air of confidence mixed with a whiff of the saloon. Our house at 11 Clove Road was nearly square and shingled top and sides. It had a hipped roof with dormers front and sides, a wraparound porch, six rooms with a maid's room on the third floor, plus attic storage. Flagstone sidewalks flanked Clove Road, as they did other streets in the neighborhood. The road had recently been paved following sewer excavations, to which my father had paid too close attention.

Whatever the source, he contracted typhoid fever, suffered a long illness, and nearly died, as I was to hear repeatedly in early childhood. His protracted illness left him in poor health and financially strapped, for medical insurance did not then exist. Fortunately, his father, William T., a prosperous and thrifty farmer, rescued us from the poorhouse. For years father suffered "sick headaches" and nausea, from job-related stress.

The "fresh air fad" dominated pediatric thinking just then. Babies were bundled and put out to air. Anyway, I contracted pneumonia. An aromatic putty called "Antiflugistine," heated as hot as the patient could stand without burning the skin, was then the sovereign remedy for reducing congestion. I still have a scar on my chest. Poultices of salt pork were thought to relieve sore throats and hoarse cough. Castor oil and cod liver oil were dreaded household staples.

The earliest sounds that I recall were those of the postman stamping his feet on the porch, his whistle blown twice, and the doorbell rung twice—a morning ritual that welcomed the day. On the stair landing one answered the telephone, a stand-up model with receiver on the hook, number 228w, which rarely rang. Of greater interest to a youngster was the mechanism of a nearby grandfather clock that struck on the hour and also marked the phases of the moon. Father had bought the clock in auction rooms on 125th Street. It had once kept time for the Pell family, one of the descendants of which traced the clock to Clove Road and yearly came to call and try to persuade father to part with it, which he finally did.

In my fourth year going on five in December, Mother persuaded Mr. Vincent, principal of the Mayflower Elementary School and himself an "upstater," to admit me to kindergarten, where my sister had preceded me the previous year. (My parents were advocates of public schools.) There I came to know Fred "Fritz" Frost, who would follow his father into architecture. One day a new boy showed up in yellow rompers; we were told he had recently come from Turkey. Born of Greek parents, he even then exhibited a classic Dinaric profile. His name was Elia Kazan. We three were destined to go through the Mayflower grades together and then four years of New Rochelle High School. Fritz Frost excelled in manual training, in which we all learned to handle tools and make birdhouses in anticipation of Arbor Day. I still recall Mr. Girard's demonstration of how to sharpen a plane and his caution not to set it down on the blade.

I no longer recall the name of a tall, gaunt teacher from Elmira College who greeted our seventh-grade year with a demonstration of how to diagram sentences. She not only made it interesting but also taught us to identify parts of speech, and we gained some notion of how the language we took for granted was constructed and worked. A believer in the oral tradition, she discovered Kazan's talent for speech, and she selected the two of us to memorize and practice famous examples of oratory and deliver them to the school assembly. My assignment was Lincoln's Gettysburg Address, which I breezed through in rehearsal—but I blew a line in performance, which I suffered through with her coaching from the back of the room. Eli, a born performer, did beautifully, as he would throughout high school.

Mayflower grammar school was virtually an outpost of upstate New York. From Union Springs on Cayuga's waters came Anna Belle Shank, who introduced us in eighth grade to English literature and poetry. Miss Shank converted Kazan into an avid reader, and he discovered New Rochelle's public library, where he borrowed books for his mother, who seldom went out in public but was improving her English. I went with him on one of his trips and took out my first library card.

Our neighborhood was not much given to reading; people were sports oriented—tennis, golf, and sailing. Baseball and football claimed an even wider following. Two blocks up Clove Road at the corner of Mayflower lived the Morton family on an ample lot where one could practice punting and kicking goals. It was a field that produced Billy Morton, a star in high school and afterward All-American at Dartmouth.

We used to pray for snow, for the great winter sport was sliding downhill on Coligni Avenue, so named by the founders of the city for a French Huguenot admiral. Bobsleds made it from the top at Webster Avenue down all four blocks to North Avenue, the north-south axis of the city, although we lesser sledders ran out of momentum at Clove Road. The greatest hazard to avoid was teams of draft horses shod with calks hauling stone uphill. I managed to run under one such team and luckily came away with only a knick on the forehead, thanks to a kindly steed and a concerned teamster. After dark at bedtime one could hear the gong on Heinie Octavec's Flexible Flyer as it sped by Clove Road and faded out toward North Avenue. The Octavec family operated a piano factory in the Bronx, an industry the family had brought from Prague, and just then pianos were in demand.

Mother played an upright model by Kranich and Bach, around which we all sang hymns and ballads from the Civil War, still favorites in the memories of my parents. None of us could match mother's rich contralto, for which she found a place in the local Choral Arts Society. Girls took piano lessons, my sister's lot, and I began violin lessons at age eleven—too late to accomplish much, especially for a boy more interested in baseball. My first teacher, Professor Steinmetz, charged less than New Rochelle's reigning maestro, a man named Grosskopf, and Herr Steinmetz came to the house. Once a week of an afternoon, when I would rather have been tossing a ball in some vacant lot, the old Prussian would open his violin case and say, "Now let's get right into the business." Bowing technique and intonation proved less difficult than finding time to practice an hour each day. My first instrument, a factory fiddle, came from Gemunder's store in New York, one of which family my parents knew through some connection in the German community. That instrument served me through high school and college.

After my two miserable performances in Professor Steinmetz's annual recitals at Germania Hall, renamed Liberty Hall in the aftermath of World War I, where none of us felt comfortable, Mother discovered Grace MacDermott, a student of Leopold Auer, who had followed his virtuoso students from St. Petersburg to the Julliard School in New York. But for a sophomore in high school, there were too many distractions, including girls and sports, for me to progress with the violin. Father recalled that he had once had Al Tenzor in class, who was then playing in various orchestras in the city, and he agreed to accept me as a student. This meant following father's route to 96th Street, descending from the El carrying a violin case, and making my way alone through the tenement district to the apartment of my new teacher. I was scared, at first, but gradually became accustomed to this not unfriendly new world where music was respected. People greeted me in passing from their stoops.

I was now in the hands of a performing musician who was determined to put me in shape. At our second session, he assigned lessons in four books—Rimally's *Scales*, Kreutzer's *Exercises*, a book on bowing techniques, and, to encourage me, Handel's *Sonatas*. These lessons went on for two years and gave me confidence: I could read music. Still, I lacked a real musical sense and never could play by ear.

Meanwhile, I played in the high-school orchestra.

Claude Bragdon, or, as students called him, "Zubu," an alumnus of Bowdoin College in Maine, held up the scholastic standard of New Rochelle High School. He invariably wore his Phi Beta Kappa key suspended from a gold chain across his ample vest as if to remind us that scholarship, rather than sports, was our real purpose as students. It was an unpopular position in a city bent on sports, especially football, but he had the support of my teacher parents. Indeed, one or two of my teachers had roomed with us, and they continually reminded me to toe the mark. I did run the half-mile with indifferent success, and I managed the football team my senior year, this in the midst of a school-wide election conducted by Dick Geoghegan, who, with typical Irish political flare, defeated my friend and rival Elia Kazan.

Sophomore year, we shared Ella Fife's geometry class up to the regents' final. Father had procured for me a set of mechanical drawing instruments, which enabled me to work out Euclid's propositions with some precision and to score one-hundred on the regents' final. Ella Fife called me to the front and kissed me, to my great embarrassment. Eli scored ninety-five, as I recall, and escaped. I did less well in Latin, which my parents insisted I endure for four years. The engineering in Caesar's Gallic Wars appealed to me, and the poetry of Virgil's *Aeneid* afforded some memorable bits. Junior year I came alive in chemistry, which was taught by a Dartmouth alumnus named Griffin, who assigned us laboratory work and then retired to his office, only to emerge in a cloud of ammonia, which suppressed the scent of alcohol. He was an excellent teacher and motivated some of us to go on to college.

Clifton T. Edgerly had come down from Yale, where making tenure proved impossible for a PhD in French. He, too, was a loyal Dartmouth alumnus, and he saw to it that several of us including Billy Morton, a talented football prospect, had special tutorials to prepare us for college-level French. A second Yale refugee, named Bartlett, perhaps attracted by a higher salary, introduced us to Chaucer's *Canterbury Tales*, encouraging us to memorize and recite whole passages. Here Kazan revealed a native talent for speech.

The Fenton Farm at Conewango

Every summer until my sixteenth year, we rented our house in New Rochelle and migrated to the family farm in southwestern New York, where we stayed until school opened after Labor Day. This return to the family roots entailed a week of packing trunks—a huge, dome-topped cavern for Mother's and the children's clothes and a steamer trunk for father in which he invariably locked the train tickets. On the day of departure, we waited for O'Brien's horse and wagon to take the trunks to the New Haven station, where we boarded the train to 125th Street, an elevated first stop out of Grand Central, where the brass of stair rails and enormous spittoons always gleamed. There we boarded the sleeper to Buffalo. The view up the Hudson to Albany from the diner afforded memorable glimpses of Bannerman's Castle and West Point. On arrival upstate in Albany, we children were put to bed in a lower berth, the window and aisle curtains drawn, although I invariably peeked out at Schenectady before sleeping on the way to Buffalo. I developed a real affection for the New York Central Railway over the years.

At Buffalo we transferred to the Buffalo and Southwestern, on which Conewango Valley was the third stop short of Jamestown, the end of the line. I recall creaky cars drawn by Mother Hubbard engines that belched cinders. These high-wheeled behemoths featured the engineer's cab halfway forward of the fire cab. Grandfather invariably met us with the surrey, drawn by "Old Fred," who was more dependable than "Old Mag," to deliver us three miles up the Flat Iron Road to the farm. Our baggage followed in a farm wagon with a team driven by a tenant farmer.

The farm comprised a north plot of some 220 original acres, then farmed by tenants, and a south plot of 80 acres that Grandfather had bought from Jim Millman in the 1880s, including a gingerbread Victorian house in the Queen Anne style and a matching horse barn across the road. It had space for the surrey and buggy and stalls for four horses. A cow barn with some twenty milking stanchions stood empty and was used to store hay, the herd of forty-some head of Holsteins being concentrated on the upper place and milked by tenants. Also unused were milk house, corn crib, chicken house, ice house, and the original farmhouse, a modified Greek-revival style building long since weathered of paint to a pleasing silvery gray. It was then used as the farm shop and for hardware storage, with an anvil for cracking butternuts. We children spent rainy days there, affectionately naming it the "funny house"—it was our favorite place.

Behind the funny house ran Butternut Creek, also called Fenton's Brook, a spring-fed stream that originated to the north in the town of Leon, crossed the road south of the house, and circled the dooryard and garden, thence west by the cow barn to its ultimate junction with the Conewango. Two huge tamarack trees bordered its banks just downstream of the bridge, yielding hideouts for enormous brown trout, which I watched from above, lying on my stomach, but never caught. Upstream the creek held brookies, of which one came down to take up residence in the pool above the cow barn and grew fat on food scraps and tossed grasshoppers. None of us had proper tackle or ever dreamed of fly fishing; de rigueur was the twelve-foot bamboo pole, a line, number eight hooks, and worms or crayfish, which the creek held in abundance. Father did take a twenty-four-inch brown trout on such a rig and fell in once or twice. The banks were eroded and slippery. Pools farther downstream held suckers, which I learned to catch by drifting bait near the bottom.

From the woodpile to the rear of the Victorian house, one could enter the cavernous cellar through a wide door, gaining access to the cider barrel on the left. Beyond it, milk and other perishables rested on the cool dirt floor. Stairs led to an enclosed woodshed and to a winter privy at the rear. The north lawn sloped up to the first floor where one entered the dining room and behind it the kitchen, where a large woodstove heated water for baths in a washtub. A pitcher pump and iron sink served to wash face and hands. A south door and porch led from the dining room down a path to the summer privy, past a plank-topped reservoir that held water piped from the Mason farm's artesian well, which Grandfather had partly financed. The pantry off the dining room, under a stairwell leading to the second floor, was off-limits to a small boy. Forward of the stairs, the living room served as farm office, where Grandfather kept his diary and accounts and greeted neighbors and tenants. A large upright stove occupied the center of the room, but its most memorable feature was its floor and wainscoting of alternating cherry and maple matched boards. My grandparents occupied an adjacent downstairs bedroom to the south, and double doors opened onto the parlor, its bay window filled with potted plants on the sunny side and its front view overlooking the flagstone walk to the gate and mailbox.

My parents occupied the front bedroom upstairs. The north bedroom, where I had a great double bed, afforded access through a floor register to conversations in the living room below when neighbors gathered evenings to rehearse battles in the Civil War, debate the merits of the Dairymen's League, or hear Grandfather recite *Marmion* and other epic poetry of Sir Walter Scott. I frequently fell asleep half hanging out of bed.

My first chore was to keep the woodbox filled. Otherwise, I was told to stay out of the kitchen. Grandfather discovered deficiencies in my Mayflower School education, which he and Uncle Will (my father's sister's husband) proceeded to repair. They found me wanting in tables of quantity—quarts in a peck, pecks in a bushel—essential in measuring feed for horses, and weak on fractions, which were faithfully recorded above the feed bins in the horse barn. Mother had a fit about my using an ax, but Grandfather demonstrated how to lop branches from a fallen tree, always putting the log between one's feet and the ax. Uncle Will taught me to mow with a scythe, keeping the heel on the ground and the point of the blade slightly elevated.

Firewood was delivered as maple slabs, which Grandfather split to kitchen size and piled neatly in cords. I watched by the hour to learn how he did it. He tilted a slab aslant of a second slab laid crosswise to absorb the blow, held the first slab with his toe, and proceeded to peel off pieces of stove wood by twisting the ax as it struck, a trick that I gradually mastered.

In 1916 Father persuaded Grandfather to buy a Buick touring car, which cost a thousand dollars, a princely sum in those days. Grandfather, having grown up driving trotters, never quite mastered the "infernal machine" and once tore down a section of fence at the milk plant in Leon. But the car enabled Father to tour the county searching for early-American furniture that had originally come to western New York by oxcart or via the Erie Canal. Such treasures had been put up in the attic or overhead in corncribs to make way for chests and dining-room sets from nearby Jamestown or Grand Rapids. These early pieces we restored in the funny house or farmed out to local craftsmen for restoration.

In the early twenties the Buick took us to the Allegany Reservation of the Seneca Nation, a drive of some twenty miles, to collect the odd splint basket and attend the Green Corn ceremonies at Coldspring Longhouse (Fenton, "Green Corn Ceremony," 1963). On these visits, the Fentons' long friendship with the family of Amos Snow immersed me in Seneca life. Amos's son Jonas lived at Allegany Reservation and worked with the "regular gang" on the Erie Railroad. Jonas and my father shared an interest in the arts, the one a carver of masks, the other a painter. After my family acquired the Buick, going to the reservation to visit the Snows and their neighbors became a favorite summer outing. Jonas's wife picked huckleberries along the Erie tracks and shared them with us. I played with the Johnny John boys while father sketched along the Allegheny River. Chauncey Johnny John, the boys' grandfather, amused my father with tales of other collectors, including George Heye, founder of the Museum of the American Indian.

Having learned to harness a buggy horse, drive a team hitched to a hayrack, and maneuver a load of hay into the barn without stripping the barn door off its track, I was prepared to drive the team on a mowing machine when Grandfather died in 1924, virtually ending our summers at Conewango Valley.

Westport, Connecticut (1926–1935)

Having settled Grandfather's estate, Father, who by this time had joined the faculty of Stuyvesant High School on the lower East Side, began looking for an early-American house in nearby Connecticut, where some of his artist friends had preceded him. He found such a house in Westport, where taxes were then reasonable, schools were adequate for my younger brother, and there was train service to Father's work in the city. The house on East State Street had been built by a sea captain named Fairchild early in the nineteenth century. He evidently employed ship carpenters to fashion the interior woodwork, even to the extent of hinged paneled doors on three fireplaces. The dining-room hearth included a Dutch oven, and in a remote wing, the fireplace of what we called the "summer kitchen"—perhaps the kitchen of the original house—also had an oven.

The summer kitchen held a mystery that we never solved. A trapdoor in the corner toward the Boston Post Road accessed a stone-walled chamber leading to a similar tunnel that diminished to crawl space as it led down beneath the lawn toward the carriage entrance. Father forbade our exploring the passage: it might have led to an open well; we might get trapped or suffocated. But eventually temptation overcame me, and I explored the passage to where I could still turn around, without solving the mystery. A local theory held that 244 East State Street was a stop on the Underground Railroad. I was too preoccupied with graduate work just then to follow up on this lead, and I soon left Westport.

Upstairs of the original east wing, the roof came down to eaves above two "lie on your stomach" front windows that provided the only daylight. To provide headroom for a bedroom, hall, and bathroom, a rough carpenter named Fred Reichert, whom Father had known in New Rochelle, raised a dormer over each front window and one on the back for headroom in the bathroom. Previous residents had coped. After installing bath and furnace, we moved in that summer of 1925. Meanwhile, sister Frances had gone off to Connecticut College for Women, while I stayed behind in New Rochelle to finish high school, rooming with friends of the family named Worth, also from upstate New York, near Utica.

Graduation separated me from friends. Fritz Frost entered Princeton. Eli Kazan and I received scholarships to Williams, but I was also awarded scholarship aid, dependent on grades, at Dartmouth, which I accepted, hoping to wait tables and seek other employment to ease the burden on parents who were supporting two children in private colleges. Father suggested Columbia and living at home or, better yet, City College of New York, where as a city employee he could seek free tuition. But my mind was made up.

That first summer in Westport I joined a crew of house painters as an apprentice. We worked on eighteenth-century buildings bordering the harbor at South Norwalk, where I was put to stripping windows, commonly eight over twelve panes of glass. The older men in the crew had painted for years with Dutch Boy white lead. Their hands shook, and they could no longer see or control a brush. My employment lasted until the painters' summer picnic on Huckleberry Island—a glorious drink fest in late August.

Everett Bulkley of Southport, seasoned member of Dartmouth class of 1929, discovered that Bob Chittim of Norwalk and I would matriculate that fall. The lone son of a marine hardware merchant in South Norwalk, Everett tooled the shore towns in a Model-T open Ford, black with red wheels, and he offered to drive us to Hanover, New Hampshire, and share expenses. That memorable journey up the Connecticut River valley past Northampton, the weekend destination of so many Dartmouth undergraduates, crossed toll bridges and passed through one-way railroad underpasses to White River Junction and Hanover. The road to Northampton would claim the lives of too many of our contemporaries until Federal Highway 95 superseded it. Just then it was a lark.

Dartmouth College

I arrived in Hanover with an old suitcase, a laundry case, a violin, and a pair of worn track shoes. I had hoped to land a spot in the freshman commons orchestra, which meant free meals, but George

Fredrickson of Worcester had already preempted the violin chair. Classmates with better connections had the pick of the eating-club jobs; waiter jobs had been allotted to athletes. In desperation I sought a kitchen job in the Main Street greasy spoons, where second semester I landed a job washing dishes evenings in Scotty's Cafe. My coworker was a black upperclassman named Wormley, who taught me the drill. He was obviously bright and would later score one-hundred on the anatomy final in medical school. I have often wondered what happened to him.

For a brief moment I attracted some notice on the track at Memorial Field. Someone suggested that I enter the freshman track meet, which Harry Hillman and Harvey Cohn had devised to discover talent for later track teams. Having run the eight-eighty in high school, I opted for and won the gold medal in the thousand yards against weak competition. Hillman criticized my form, saying that I would have to build up my shoulders and learn how to use my arms, and he recommended that I report to Pat Kearny in the gym. I should meanwhile report for track practice. The next week he found two middle-distance runners, upperclassmen who regularly ran two-minute half-miles (my best time up to then was two minutes, ten seconds). His two regulars promptly left me in the ruck eating cinders, and I came in far behind. I did not yet know that the Lathem twins, who had starred at Andover in the Boston Mechanics Hall meets, were out for freshman football and would soon add to my misery. I did report for track practice for nearly two years before I discovered other activities outdoors in winter and on the river in spring. Fraternities suddenly lost interest in me.

With all this random activity, grades suffered, and I ended freshman year with a string of cs. I was continually strapped for funds. Housework for faculty wives paid forty cents per hour. Professor Marsden of Thayer School and his wife, Mary, kept me in pin money.

One redeeming feature of that year was playing in the orchestra of the Handel Society, which met for rehearsals Sunday evenings in the basement of Webster Hall, then the sole auditorium of the college. The orchestra embraced faculty, undergraduates, and townspeople. I played in the second violin section and gradually moved up to the first desk of that section in later years. To my right sat John Merrill Poor, college astronomer and clarinet player, who invariably grumbled, "That damned priest with his box," when the pastor of the White Church came in late from evening prayer service holding his cello overhead.

Professor Silverman, of mathematics, an accomplished musician, headed the viola section, and western historian Robert Riegel, as concertmaster, led the first violins, along with Dud Goldman ('29), while my classmates Manny Glass and George Fredrickson held the second desk.

At some point conductor Maurice Longhurst invited me to accompany several faculty members of the orchestra for coffee after rehearsal. We met in the backroom of Saia's Grocery on Main Street. The coffee was awful, but I soon learned that faculty were human beings with all the faults and virtues of the rest of us.

The Handel Society gave one or two concerts a year, for which we prepared at length. We lacked key instruments and competent players for a full orchestra, but someone had left funds to bring in "ringers," and so members of the Boston Symphony Orchestra (bso) appeared on the eve of our concerts and distributed themselves at crucial spots—the woodwinds, the first and second violin desks. One year I had the good fortune to sit with a Dutch violinist named Haage who had played the Beethoven symphony that we were then rehearsing innumerable times and knew it by heart. He taught me how to bring out the nuances at various points and advised me to play, in the rapid movements, every first note in the bar, and he would play the rest.

In the 1930s, when I was stationed in western New York for the U.S. Indian Service, the bso came to Rochester, and I attended the concert with my fiancée. I spotted old friends in the violin sections and went backstage at intermission to greet them. Two veterans of the Handel Society concerts proceeded to introduce me to other members of the orchestra and recall their own Hanover experiences. Although I have ceased to play, I enjoy attending bso rehearsals at Tanglewood and watching the orchestra work.

Distributive requirements specified a course in the natural sciences sophomore year. Choice lay among chemistry, physics, and astronomy. "Cheerless" Richardson (chemistry) had the reputation of screening students for medical school; Gordon Ferry Hull, an eminent physicist, was known to be tough; and John Merrill Poor, college astronomer, famed for his wit, gave a "pipe" course and failed no one. Such was the talk at track practice of a May afternoon. Since I already knew Professor Poor from the Handel Society, I called on him at Shattuck Observatory, where I found him in a welter of calculations and papers spread all over the floor. He urged me to sign up for advanced math and physics but relented and admitted me to Astronomy 1.

At the first meeting of the class, he mentioned that the college bookstore might have a few copies of Russell, Dugan, and Stewart's *Celestial Astronomy*, the text for the course. I found a copy and began to read it along with the lectures and demonstrations, to discover that whole sections dealt with the history of science, which fascinated me, from the Arabs to Ptolemy, Copernicus, Tycho Brahe, Kepler, and Isaac Newton. This was my dish. Poor allowed that he often talked in other people's sleep. There was never enough time before the bell for nine o'clock classes to finish his calculations, which stretched frequently to all sides of the room. He would protest that one day we would simply ignore time and finish the problem or found a college without schedules. In late October, he told us that the college registrar insisted that he turn in midsemester grades; he announced an hour exam. The following Monday as he distributed the blue books, he remarked that he wanted to see two of us after class—Fenton and one other. Classmates hung around to learn what I had done. "You read the book. If you are seriously interested in astronomy, go take physics with Professor Hull and mathematics, and when you graduate I will send you to Shapley at Harvard." I got my first A at Dartmouth in Professor Poor's course.

Junior year I met European thought in the lectures of W. K. Stewart and the nature writers and types of rebel thought under Herbert Faulkner West, who converted rowdy athletes into lifelong book collectors and created the Friends of the Dartmouth Library to house their harvest. But it was McQuilkin DeGrange's "Search for Social Law" from Aristotle to Auguste Compte and the "Positivists" that really challenged me. Because of it, I read the originals in the new Baker Library, where I first encountered Franz Boas's *The Mind of Primitive Man* and Edward Sapir's *Language* while browsing in the Tower Room. Hard as I worked, I received only eighties and the odd ninety on DeGrange's weekly quizzes, while two seniors who sat behind me—John Dickey (afterward president of the college) and Leonard Doob (later Sterling Professor of Psychology at Yale)—consistently scored nineties.

By junior year, my financial troubles were largely over. I clerked in the Dartmouth Co-op, which sold everything from books to skis, and waited on a table of Phi Psi's at the Green Lantern for lunch and dinner, having graduated from faculty household chores at forty cents an hour. My grades were up and so was my scholarship. Summers in Westport I served as assistant to Frank Dayton, superintendent of Compo Beach, which entailed renting bathhouses and similar duties that left me time to read. The beach was free to Westport residents, but bathers from Wilton, Weston, and neighboring townships were obliged to rent by the hour. These out-of-towners included some famous literati—Padraic and Mary Colum, for example, and the Shakespearean actor Walter Hamden and his family. Mary Colum caught me reading one day and afterward brought me books. Mondays, when the Compo Beach Volunteer Lifeguards were at work in the city, I did lifeguard duty. Among others, I rescued Hamden's mentally handicapped daughter, who got caught between tides. I soon learned that the public can be ungrateful; one victim threatened to sue the town because she alleged that in bringing her in, I pulled her hair.

Westport in the 1920s was loaded with talent both in the arts and in letters. At the beach I knew Chilly Brooks, son of the literary historian Van Wyck Brooks. Junior year, when I happened to meet Chilly in the village and mentioned that I was writing an essay on Thoreau's views on education for a contest (Herb West had persuaded the Mandel Brothers of Chicago to underwrite prizes), Chilly reminded me that his father knew a lot about Thoreau and that I should talk with him. Somehow, spring vacation slipped by without my seeing Mr. Brooks. I had gone through the Thoreau *Journals* and had read *Walden, A Week on the Concord and Merrimack Rivers, The Maine Woods,* and *Cape Cod;* I needed to get on with the writing. Faculty readers said I had included too much of Thoreau and not enough of my own ideas. I should have seen Mr. Brooks. I received second prize.

Dartmouth enables seniors in good standing to combine their fourth year with a year of graduate work in medicine, engineering, or business administration, which suffices for a major, and then go on to a fifth year of graduate work in their chosen field. I was admitted to the Amos Tuck School of Business Administration and Finance in the autumn of the 1929 stock market crash and lasted until midway of the second semester. I found the courses neither challenging nor pertinent to the times, and I did poorly in all except marketing. From dean's list to probation in a single year marked the decline in my fortunes. In desperation I called on Craven Leacock, dean of the faculty, who greeted me, my record in hand, with: "Fenton, anyone who can score three-point in Dartmouth College can have anything he wants in this office. What is your problem?" I told him that I had been dismissed from Tuck School and wanted to repeat my senior year. The dean responded that as an undergraduate I still remained under his jurisdiction as a member of the college. I could return in September, but without a scholarship. I mentioned an interest in anthropology, which prompted him to tell me that Bob McKennan (class of '25) was returning from Harvard, having completed the PhD under Roland B. Dixon, and would be offering courses in the sociology department. I did not then know that Bob had married the dean's daughter.

The year had not been a total loss. I won the singles in the Ledyard Canoe Club regatta and the doubles with Warren Parrish, with whom I had made the five-day voyage to the sea the previous June, and I had served as treasurer of the club for two years. The club owned some railroad shares, the beneficence of the Reverend John E. Johnson of Pennsylvania, the returns of which we used to replace the fleet of canoes. Discovering that the college treasurer, Halsey T. Edgerton, took a dim view of undergraduate clubs holding securities not within his control, I went to see him and pled the cause for a new boathouse to replace the existing green shed, which was beyond repair. When I mentioned the securities and told him that Gene Magenau was prepared to draw up plans for a structure that would meet the club's needs, Mr. Edgerton allowed that if the club would sign over the securities to the college, he would undertake to finance a new building. Mr. Edgerton soon became deeply involved in directing club workers clearing the site and in supervising construction. Perhaps my success forecast a career in organizing scholarship.

A year under Bob McKennan's tutelage, in which I wrote a senior essay on the roots of Iroquois culture, prepared me for graduate work in anthropology. My first choice was Harvard, in order to work under Roland B. Dixon, McKennan's mentor, but there were no fellowships available to first-year students.

I passed the summer after graduation passed as a counselor to the children of the Yelping Hill colony, the summer retreat of the

Saturday Review of Literature families and friends at West Cornwall, Connecticut. Between taking the children swimming and on canoe trips on the Housatonic River, I shared meals and was invited evenings to the homes of the members, who included the presidents of Vassar and Wesleyan. Henry Noble McCracken listened to my discussion of migration theories and aboriginal succession in New York State, and his daughter Maisry accompanied me to Music Mountain for chamber music. "Lady" Canby (Mrs. Henry Seidel Canby) persuaded me to review a book on boys' camping for the *Saturday Review,* my first venture in print.[2] West Cornwall was oriented toward New Haven.

Father, through colleagues, got me an interview in September with Clark Wissler, curator of anthropology at the American Museum of Natural History, who came up weekly to Yale's Institute of Human Relations to direct the research of some graduate students. Wissler recognized me as an undergraduate who had come into the museum to consult him on a career in anthropology. After listening to my plea, Wissler picked up the phone and then directed me to the dean of the graduate school, Wilbur Cross, in Connecticut Hall. Dean Cross asked me where I had gone to college and examined my transcript. "What were you doing freshman year, playing football?" After I told him that I was out for track and trying to find an eating-club job, he remarked, "I like a transcript like this. You improved." That was how I was admitted to graduate school at Yale, before the day of the Graduate Records Examination.

That same day I learned that Edward Sapir was coming that fall from Chicago as Sterling Professor to head the new Department of Anthropology. I had money to sign up for two courses: ethnology, under George Peter Murdock, and prehistory, with Cornelius Osgood, a Chicago PhD. I planned to live at home and commute to New Haven from Westport.

1. 11 Cove Road, New Rochelle, New York.

2. Frances and William Fenton, 1910.

3. Victorian farmhouse at Conewango, New York.

4. Helene Mason, Frances, and William Fenton at the farm.

5. John W. Fenton with brown trout.

TWO

At Yale and among the Senecas

My introduction to graduate work at Yale immersed me in two realms, ethnology and prehistory. George Peter Murdock, a consummate bibliographer who could hand each student references on any ethnographic topic complete with call numbers, assigned topics to each of his graduate students together with a specific reading list. Each student was expected to produce an ethnographic essay on that topic by the end of the semester. My assignment was the Indians of Connecticut. J. W. DeForest, as an undergraduate, had written a book on the subject in the preceding century, and still earlier Ezra Stiles, a future Yale president, had mapped floor plans of native wigwams. At the end of the semester, Professor Murdock had me read my essay to the seminar. He both praised and critiqued my writing, telling me to use active verbs and avoid the passive voice. Murdock was a comprehensive teacher (serving on my doctoral committee), like most at that time not welcoming to women at Yale, and known for gatherings at his home in Hamden. Being a commuter, I unfortunately missed most of the latter.

Clark Wissler had advised me to come see him, when I was ready to pursue graduate work, at the Institute of Human Relations at Yale where he spent two or three days a week. Wissler and I commuted to New Haven, he from New York, and I from Westport. Going home Friday nights he frequently took me by cab to the station. During the ride to Westport I listened to anecdotes on the history of anthropology about which he was writing, which aroused my curiosity. Wissler had a keen perception of the personalities involved, their struggles, and collaborations. I count myself among Wissler's "boys." He had no sons of his own, but he embraced Jack Ewers, Harold Conklin, and me as if we were.

Prehistory under Cornelius Osgood proved a contentious experience. Only four of us signed up for the course, which Osgood gave for the first time in the shadow of George Grant MacCurdy, recently retired author of *Human Origins*, which we read. Each of us had to prove his worth, which Osgood grudgingly acknowledged. A veteran of the University of Chicago under Maynard Hutchins, he manifested disdain for the Ivy League and its alumni.

Eager for field experience, I learned that the Laboratory of Anthropology at Santa Fe offered coveted fellowships for training in fieldwork in both ethnology and archaeology. I missed out on the ethnology party under Leslie White among the Hopi. Meanwhile, I had talked with MacCurdy about joining a team in European prehistory and mentioned it to Clark Wissler. He remarked that there were no jobs in the United States for a European prehistorian; instead, he urged me to apply for a Laboratory of Anthropology fellowship in archaeology under William Duncan Strong of the Smithsonian Institution (si), who would be working on the Great Plains of Nebraska and South Dakota. He also said that I should read the literature on western exploration and Pawnee and Arikara ethnology and that he would write the committee.

That summer of 1932 on the plains proved a wise decision. Everyone of consequence in Plains Indian studies visited our site at Signal Butte and later the Leavenworth site at Standing Rock Reservation on the Missouri River. Matthew W. Stirling, director of the Bureau of American Ethnology, joined us for a week in camp on the Missouri. An elderly Dakota named Crazy Bear rode his horse down to inspect our dig most days. On occasion he brought an interpreter. He apparently reveled in our digging up the cultural remains of the "Rees" (Arikaras). I began to quiz him about artifacts that surfaced in storage pits. One day I found cut and incised bison ribs, which he explained had once held feathers to guide them when cast to glide upon snow, which I immediately linked to the Iroquois game of "snow snake." I commenced to think that field ethnology was more rewarding than archaeology.

The second year of graduate school went better. I received the Carroll Cutler Fellowship, which paid tuition, provided for books, and defrayed commuting expenses. I carried a full load of courses, notably Wissler on the direct historical approach to Plains Indian cultures; Te Rangi Hiroa—Sir Peter Buck, the Maori physician, statesman, and self-made anthropologist from New Zealand— on Polynesian material culture; and Edward Sapir on phonetics with native informants and his seminar on social organization. Having directed a research program on the Six Nations Reserve, an Iroquois community near Brantford, Ontario, while director of the Anthropological Survey of Canada from 1910 to 1925, Sapir put me to reading and reporting on the Iroquois League. I discovered that it worked by projecting initial patterns of social organization onto higher levels of integration. I also learned that keeping the presentation moving before Sapir interjected questions was key. It was one of my better efforts.

Following my presentation, Sapir took me aside and told me that he had funds for my fieldwork, and he inquired where I proposed to begin. When I mentioned my family's connection with the Snow family of the Seneca Nation, we agreed that I should start at Allegany. He advised finding a field of concentration early so that I should have a subject for a dissertation and not just field notes. He thought I might find a beginning in clan organization in the context of ceremonialism. "Don't just collect stories," he advised.

I had attended Sapir's seminar on phonetics, but the Seneca language would be new to me. To get me started, he loaned me a copy of *Phonetic Transcription of American Indian Languages*, of which he was joint author. These hints would prove a boon to a novice fieldworker, but I soon found out that the Senecas would control my learning and that their interests would govern its progress.[1]

Among the Senecas

Snow Street was a shortcut connecting Highway 17 from Steamburg east to the road north from Quaker Bridge, which passed the Coldspring Longhouse, forming a triangle within which most of the community activity took place. That first summer I set up a tent in Jonas Snow's dooryard and became an adjunct to his household.

From this vantage point I kept a journal, a miscellany of family life, medicines, rattlesnakes, turtles, drunks, feuds, friends, ballgames, singing society sessions, mutual-aid activities, and socials at the Longhouse. It was all quite confusing at first.

My progress was affected more by accident than by the good advice of my professors or the strategy I had devised for my fieldwork. Members of the Snow family were helpful in sorting out the bits and pieces that came to me all at once, but they had concerns of their own that left little time for my queries. They included me in their activities whenever they could.

Formal work on medicines with an informant yielded systematic data, and by way of getting acquainted I recorded genealogies and noted the personal names of the several clans, which later enabled me to sort out participation in ceremonies.[2] But it was not these structured efforts at ethnology that were most rewarding. It was the informal, after-hours activities that I shared with members of my "family" that brought me in touch with the culture and enabled me to experience Seneca society as a going concern.

Evenings, the Snow boys, Windsor and Linus (later a World War II casualty at Saint-Lô), led me on the paths that cut through the brush to the ballground, where we fielded grounders or practiced lacrosse. Or we poled over the river in a johnboat to Crick's Run or went "torching" at night, or we swam in the gravel pit, where I taught Seneca boys the six-beat crawl. Once while returning, we stopped at a house where we heard singing. The singers sat facing each other on two rows of chairs or benches. The lead singer held a water drum and beater, with which he lined out the song, while the others kept time beating horn rattles in the palm of one hand and bumping their heels with the drumbeats. Then they repeated the song together, drum and rattles vibrato, while maintaining the slower tempo with their heels. The songs belonged to the Enskanye: repertoire of the Women's Shuffle Dance, I was told. The singers made up a mutual-aid society that performed charitable work in the Coldspring community. The hostess passed me a brimming bowl of corn soup, saying, "His face is white, but maybe he likes soup. Perhaps later he may learn to sing."

Presently, the leader, Albert Jones of the Snipe Clan, then married to Jonas Snow's sister of the Hawk Clan, having gathered the horn rattles and put them with the drum in a handbasket, paused at the door to say to me, "We are glad that you came. You are welcome to sit with us. We will let you know where we next meet."

I would soon learn that singing societies were found in other Iroquois communities as well. Learning to sing that summer at Coldspring afforded me a passport later at Tonawanda and Six Nations, for the drum is to the Iroquois what the violin is to the gypsy.

People soon asked me what clan I was going to join. They assumed it would be the Hawk Clan—that of Jonas Snow; his sisters, Alice Jones and Emma Turkey; and their children, including Emma's daughter, Clara Redeye, my interpreter. The question came from two members of the Snipe Clan who were married to Hawks. The Hawk Clan was the logical choice, although I sensed that the Snipes would accept me, too.

The Hawk Clan regarded my beat-up station wagon as a means of transportation. On a Sunday "my" family decided to visit relatives at Cattaraugus and attend the lacrosse match at Pine Woods. My vehicle served as Jonas picked up friends and relatives, introducing me to the elite of Seneca informants. We stopped at a log house, the home of Jonas's mother's sister. Victim of several strokes, the old woman was bedridden, but she seemed especially glad to see me. When Jonas explained my family connection, her face brightened. I thought she said she was the one born in the shanty on the hemlock ridge, but I later learned I was mistaken. She surely knew of the incident, though. Whatever this visit meant to the members of Jonas's mother's family, to me it represented a symbolic reinforcement of the link between the Fenton family and the Senecas. I was beginning to find it difficult to sort out my role as an anthropologist from my role in my adoptive family.

My involvement in the affairs and concerns of the Hawk Clan intensified during the next two months. As the Green Corn Festival approached in late August, the sisters of Jonas Snow talked of giving me an Indian name. Formal adoption in the Hawk Clan would establish my place in the community. But for some reason they did not get around to naming me at Green Corn, which postponed my formal adoption until I returned at Midwinter. The third day of Green Corn and the eighth day of the nine-day Midwinter Festival, or Indian New Year, are the two times names are announced or changed for adults. But even that date was postponed when Jonas's mother's sister, the old woman we had visited in early summer, died in September. I drove the family to the Longhouse funeral in Newtown, on the Cattaraugus reservation, and was treated as next of kin.

One July evening in the summer of 1933, as I wrote in my journal on Snow Street, I heard Indian songs coming from the north, across the Erie tracks. When I asked the Snow family, "Who is that singing?" I was told, "That's Johnson Jimmerson practicing his songs. He wants to learn." Johnson was then a lad of fifteen, some ten years my junior, and it was soon apparent that his eagerness to master and perform the ceremonial songs amused the older, accomplished singers almost as much as my stumbling effort to acquire the Seneca language.

At the suggestion of George Herzog, then at Yale, I had brought an Edison wax cylinder recorder (for then such recording devices were the only ones available) and found Coldspring singers willing to sing their social dance songs into the metal horn. Johnson frequently attended these sessions. In a sense, he and I were both beginners, although he spoke Seneca as a first language. But the old people had not yet accepted Johnson as a singer. Instead of encouraging him, they ridiculed his efforts.

Somehow Johnson and I became friends. Perhaps it was evenings at the ballground, going to the river, or swimming at the gravel pit—activities that required little verbal communication. His maternal grandmother, Esther Fatty of the Hawk Clan, was one of four "head ones" in the Longhouse, representing her moiety of clans, so Johnson should have been well connected. But his maternal grandfather, who specialized in making bent-willow chairs, told me that Johnson was the orphaned son of a deceased daughter, with no known father. Here was the classic theme of "Thrownaway" in Seneca folklore: the fatherless boy, living on the margins, ridiculed by his elders but avid to learn—the outcast who would grow up to become a leading ritualist among his people.

And that is what happened. Years later Johnson found a girl at Cattaraugus. The war intervened. Johnson returned and raised a family. He became speaker of the Newtown Longhouse, having mastered everything of consequence in the Coldspring cycle of ceremonies, including the formal speeches and announcements.

At the moon of Midwinter 1968, I returned to witness the ceremonies at the new Coldspring Longhouse. The sixth night of the festival, or "Husk Face night," always brings visitors from Cattaraugus, Tonawanda, and sometimes Six Nations. I spotted Johnson in the crowd. We had not seen each other in years. The winner of the impromptu dancing contest among the False Face beggars that night, by acclaim, proved to be Johnson's son, whom he proudly brought over to meet me. I was fascinated to witness the learning that a father had transmitted to his son. Johnson had indeed to use his words, "raised him right." Thrownaway of our youth at Coldspring had become a *hodiont,* or faithkeeper, in the Newtown Longhouse and a leader in the singing society where he now lived. We did not meet again. It really sent me back to Snow Street when I read of Johnson's passing in 1984.

It would have been amiss to expect that other lineages of the Hawk Clan, in addition to Jonas Snow's sister's lineage, to which he belonged, would accept me that first summer at Coldspring. Esther Fatty expressed her doubts to Jonas Snow and his sisters. Old John Jimmerson opposed my activities as an ethnologist on the floor of the Longhouse, which prompted his senior, John "Twenty Canoes" Jacobs, of the Bear Clan, with whom I had been working, to remind the elders that at least I listened, whereas other young people ignored them, and it was evident that "This young man thinks what we do is worthwhile."

It was late in August 1934 before John Jimmerson began to take me seriously and allowed me to climb High Bank for tutorials from his rocking chair. At best he was a difficult, though learned, informant. His youngest son, Avery, then a lad approaching twenty, lived at home with his father. Avery liked to draw, and during one of my High Bank visits presented me with a pencil sketch of a Seneca masked dancer, which showed a considerable talent that he later converted to carving. Within a few years Avery would become the master carver of his generation (see Fenton, *False Faces,* 1987).

From opposition John had moved to a guarded rapport. When, after Green Corn, he decided to attend the renewal at Newtown of the "Little Water Medicine," the quintessential sacred rite in the Seneca cycle, he suspended doubts about me, since I had a car. It was the first time among many such all-night sessions that I would hear the complete repertoire of songs.

It was far easier to work within the lineage of Jonas Snow's elder sister, Emma Turkey. With her daughter, Clara Redeye, as interpreter; Clara's spouse, Sherman Redeye (Snipe Clan), as intermediary; and his father, Henry Redeye (Bear Clan) as primary source, I was able to undertake systematic work on the ceremonies that first year. Henry was speaker of the Coldspring Longhouse, a preacher of the "Good Message," or Handsome Lake religion, and a master of the old forms. Sherman could fill in for him at any time. This would be my team the following year.

My formal adoption into the Hawk Clan took place on January 26, 1934, at Coldspring Longhouse of the Seneca Nation. The naming of adults occurs on the eighth day of the Midwinter Festival during the celebration of *adonwen*ʔ (personal chant), which is the third of the Four Sacred Ceremonies prescribed by the prophet Handsome Lake. (The other three are the Great Feather Dance, the Drum Dance, and the Great Bowl Game. Each has its day, as at Green Corn.)[3]

Before a person is adopted, he must first be accepted by a clan, which is the basic unit of Seneca society. After being advanced by a particular maternal family and accepted by its clan relatives, one is taken into the larger, local group or community, which is composed of the segments of eight clans. A public ceremony at the Longhouse sanctions adoption. Ultimately, other Seneca communities recognize such actions.

The adoptee has a certain amount of choice. I recall that the previous summer Albert Jones (Snipe Clan), then spouse of my Hawk Clan sponsor's sister, advised me: "You must decide what clan you want to join." He was prepared to put me up in the Snipe Clan. Sherman Redeye was ready to second it. Although I was never told, I surmise that Clara Redeye had advanced my candidacy with her mother, the elder sister of Jonas Snow, my host that first summer, whom she persuaded to sponsor me as a Hawk. The matter had been agreed upon at a family feast in my honor that was held the previous summer.

A Seneca man is privileged to grant a personal name that belongs to his clan—a name that he has abandoned and that is free—to an outsider whom the clan wishes to adopt and whom he will sponsor. Jonas Snow (Hononwiyaʔgon, "He parts the riffles") of the Hawk Clan, who took me into his household in the summer of 1933, had formerly held the name Howanʔneyao, "He loses a game or wager." The name was now free, and he wished to give it to me. Jonas was at the Longhouse on the eighth morning. An adoptee may have, in addition to a sponsor, a "friend" or two *(hon-ondeoshon*ʔ*)* as additional sponsors, and such people need not be of the clan of the adoptee. Albert Jones (Snipe Clan), husband of Jonas Snow's sister Alice, would be my friend. Albert had been an invaluable help to my first fieldwork.

Having secured the permission of the two head male Longhouse officers—Levi Snow (Heron Clan) and Reuben White (Bear Clan)—who are of opposite moieties, Jonas and Albert asked the speaker, Henry Redeye (Bear Clan), to announce that Hononwiya?gon (Jonas Snow) was giving me his boyhood name. Albert (Hanojenen?s), as "conductor," directed Jonas and me to sit together on the north end of the singers' bench, facing west toward the headmen.

The formal speech of adoption is called simply "Giving a name," *howonseno:a?*. Phrasing depends on the speaker. Sherman and Clara Redeye recaptured the text for me. It follows in English:

> As it has happened in the past, names have been given to white men. That is the reason that the Hawk Clan decided to award a name belonging to that clan, namely the Hawk Clan, whom we call Hodiswen?gayo?, "the striped kind." The name that they have given, which shall be his name, is Howan?neyao. That is what you shall call him, the person whom you see here present, for he has come from the other side of New York. Here you see him where we have gathered (in this meeting). He also thinks that it amounts to something, for so he says. And that is all.

Following the nomination speech, the two sponsors—the former holder of the name and my friend—stood me up and alternately performed *adonwen?* in my honor, marching me in measured cadence the length of the Longhouse toward the women's side and returning, while chanting. Each man sang his personal song. Albert Jones had a powerful voice. One or two other men repeated the gesture. Shortly thereafter Sherman Redeye taught me to sing a personal song of my own for such occasions. The text says, "Snipe woke me. / Yeah, the Great Snipe woke me."

The nomination confirmed, a Longhouse officer, usually a friend of the candidate, asks the adoptee and his sponsor to rise and accept pledges of friendship from the people. First, the women of the clan file by and shake hands with their new clansman. The men of the clan follow. The women may say anything they wish, such as, "*Nia:wenh ske:non* (Thanks, you are well?)," to which the initiate may reply, "*Do:gens* (Indeed)." This is the ordinary greeting between friends. Another person may inquire whether the initiate knows his name, ask him to repeat it, and then tell him that that shall be his name until the old people change it, he assumes a new office, or he dies. All of this, and perhaps more, was said to me, Clara Redeye afterward told me.

Next, the "head ones" of the Longhouse—two women and two men of opposite moieties—followed by lesser officers, congratulate their new tribesman. In each rank the women take precedence over the men.

After these persons of exalted names, anyone may greet the adoptee. Sometimes a friend will approach him and say, in a joking way, "You are a bad Indian, but if you are as bad as I am, everyone knows that you will be a pretty bad Indian." Then, in a serious vein, the joker may ask the recipient to address his new relatives, pledging his loyalty to them and his devotion in times of hardship. He must remember that whenever there are ceremonies at the Longhouse, he should contribute. But it is not required that the recipient acknowledge the honor with a speech.

In following years I would learn more of the obligations of clanship, its benefits, and its demands. The name given me followed or preceded me everywhere I went among the Iroquois people. The name remained years later when I stayed away. In the words of a recent correspondent, "My Gram gave you that name in a ceremony many years ago. You can never be un-adopted!"

Among the Anthropologists Again

Leslie Spier, ethnographer extraordinary, joined the faculty in 1933–34. By that time, Frank Speck at the University of Pennsylvania had become my fieldwork mentor, but Spier did teach several of us what it meant to become professional anthropologists. Having published *Havasupai Ethnography* (1928), he was then writing *Yuman Tribes of the Gila River* (1933). There were conflicts in his data that he had yet to resolve; he would hand the information to one of us and say, "See what you can make of this." Sometimes he accepted our recommendations; otherwise, he would explain why not. Spier offered a bag-lunch seminar called "Kinship without a Headache"—a blackboard demonstration of various native North American kinship systems. He prepared me for the oral examination that May: "Just read Boas on 'Anthropology' in the *Encyclopaedia of the Social Sciences*," he advised me. It was a pity that Spier was denied tenure at Yale. He followed W. W. (Nibs) Hill to New Mexico and soon was elected to the National Academy of Sciences. Yale had missed out.

One day, talking with Peter Buck about his upcoming research on the Captain Cook Collection in the British Museum, I mentioned the upcoming orals. Buck suggested my calling on other faculty to discover their own research interests of the moment. He predicted that questions on the exam would reflect these interests. He was right. I passed the orals with distinction.

Ruth Benedict and Margaret Mead ran a seminar on "Competition and Cooperation in Primitive Societies" for their students at Columbia, each of whom worked up the material on a culture. Buell Quain had read the literature on the Iroquois, and I was invited to work with him and appear in the seminar. While waiting for the seminar to convene, I was talking with Al Lesser, whom I already knew, when Franz Boas opened his office door and summoned me inside. "Edward [Sapir] told me about you," he said. "What have you learned about Iroquois verbs?" Boas had published a note on the subject based on information he had collected from Mohawks during a train trip from Montreal to New York. I admitted that I had made small progress with the Seneca language.

On another occasion when the anthropologists and folklorists met at Yale, Boas stood after dinner, while we students sat on the floor of the Graduates Club, and delivered without a note or a misplaced word an account of a century of folklore research in America. It was an extraordinary performance.

Sapir suggested that we students form an anthropology club and asked me to organize it. Finding speakers for monthly meetings proved easy because all of the great names came to New Haven to visit Sapir and accepted our invitations to address the club. The Sapirs included us in their evenings at home. I recall first meeting A. L. Kroeber at Sapir's when he singled me out and quizzed me on my Seneca research, as if to probe the depths of my mind.

Bronislaw Malinowski was then lecturing at Cornell. I wrote to him and invited him to address the club on his view of functionalism, which was the current fad in anthropology. He replied proposing a debate: that the author of functionalism be bastinadoed and hung at sunset. I didn't understand him and thought he was kidding. But the day of his arrival he still insisted that a protagonist of the historical method speak first. All of the Yale faculty in anthropology and some others had turned out to hear him, and there I was presiding over a debate that would not start and at a loss what to do. Neither Wissler nor Spier would budge, but Peter Buck, assuming his role as a Maori, came to my rescue by contrasting the merits of interpreting Maori culture by the historical method and by the functionalist approach. That evening at Sapir's, when I asked Malinowski to explain his method to me, he turned my query around and asked me to tell him what I understood of it.

A. R. Radcliffe-Brown, the other leading functionalist, then at Chicago, came to New Haven at the invitation of some other Yale group. We managed to coopt him for the Anthropology Club. Following a dinner in his honor, he showed up at the Hall of Graduate Studies resplendent in white tie and tails. I no longer recall what he said, except that he went out of his way to berate Clark Wissler for his area approach to culture, which Wissler was no longer advocating. It was another rough evening. He made no converts.

By this time we were in the depths of the Great Depression, the department had run out of available fellowships, and there were no jobs. The New Deal was in full swing, and the federal Indian commissioner, John Collier, was conducting a revolution in Indian affairs. We invited him to address the Anthropology Club, and he accepted. Just then anthropology was in favor in the U.S. Indian Service, and Collier held that anthropologists could contribute to tribal reorganization and the writing of charters. His model was that of British social anthropologists serving the colonial administration of Africa. Just then William Duncan Strong, of the Bureau of American Ethnology, was acting in a liaison capacity to the Indian Service, and he had already directed inquiries to me in the field about the viability of the Iroquois Confederacy. Collier came to New Haven in the fall of 1934. His plan for the reorganization of Indian tribal governments provoked a lively discussion. His idea of employing anthropologists in the Indian Service received a mixed reception. Placing students had become difficult, but a career in the Indian Service was scarcely consistent with our training. Collier returned to Washington, and we all forgot about it.

U.S. Indian Service (1935–1937)

Without warning I received a telegram signed by John Collier: Would I accept the post of superintendent of the New York Indian Agency? When could I report? For years the New York agency, which represented the federal presence in Indian affairs among the reservations of the Six Nations in New York State, had occupied the attention of a part-time agent, a Salamanca Republican lawyer named W. K. Harrison. Collier evidently intended to make it a full-time job and replace the incumbent. At age twenty-six, and all-but-dissertation, I was scarcely prepared to take on an administrative post. My father offered a solution. Obviously, someone had made a mistake. I should request an interview and go to Washington. He predicted that the minute I walked into the Indian Service offices, someone would realize that the commissioner had been carried away by his Yale visit. They would probably offer me another job. And that is what happened.

The previous summer I had filed for U.S Civil Service status as "Social Worker," at the suggestion of the Yale anthropology department secretary. Previous experience coaching recreational skiing at Dartmouth, teaching canoe techniques in summer camps, and working with children at Yelping Hill, as well as jobs in the U.S. Postal Service during the Christmas rush, gained me extra points, and I emerged near the top of the list. Personnel officers in the Indian Service construed that I was qualified as "Community Worker." Would I accept a position among the Iroquois of western New York at two thousand per annum? Of course, I would need a car. Travel expense at four dollars per diem was understood. In accepting, I requested that my official station be at Akron, New York, close by Tonawanda, some sixty miles north of the agency at Salamanca, where I might begin a new kind of work apart from the Seneca Nation, among whom I had commenced fieldwork in ethnology. Tonawanda, moreover, adhered to the traditional system of life chiefs made famous by Lewis Henry Morgan in his *League of the Iroquois* (1851). I wanted to experience it at firsthand.

Having driven my old Packard roadster the length of Route 17 to Salamanca, I checked in at the New York agency, only to discover that I was not yet on the payroll and that no job description had preceded me. I reassured Special Agent Harrison that I had no designs on his job and departed the same day for Akron, my official station for nearly three years. I was going to have to design my own duties, rather than have someone in Washington or Salamanca define them for me. Having established credit with the Bank of Akron, I set out for the reservation and headed "down below" to the Longhouse community, where my sole contacts lived. I had previously worked with Jesse Cornplanter and with Elijah

David of my adopted Hawk Clan. I had attended the Handsome Lake preaching the previous year with the Coldspring Longhouse delegation. People welcomed me by my Seneca name, which had preceded me.

Not unlike other Longhouse communities, Tonawanda had a mutual-aid society, the Salt Creek Singers. They met at Jesse and Elsina Cornplanter's house, and I was invited to attend. Between songs, a speaker announced that the society would meet Sunday to cut wood for a certain widow, and he welcomed me to join them.

There was snow underfoot. Akron Hardware outfitted me with rubber boots, an ax, and a lumberjack shirt, the prevailing reservation garb, in which I was prepared to exercise skills learned as a boy on the family farm. Toward the end of winter, people were exhausted, colds were rife, and pneumonia and death struck several Longhouse families. The singing society was caught up in funeral arrangements and called on me to arrange credit for lumber with which to build coffins. I even persuaded the Social Welfare Department to pay the bills. This outraged local funeral directors, who counted on welfare funerals on the reservation as part of their income. Accommodating Indian customs must have been a New Deal plot!

Two Hawk Clan families expected me to sit through wakes that went on for several nights while the two moieties played the Delaware moccasin game to stay awake until dawn. The songs still ring in my head and surface in similar circumstances.

It soon dawned on me that my job was simply to assist the Tonawanda community in its endeavors. Field Day was the big summer event and fundraiser, and baseball and lacrosse were the current attractions. The planning committee invited me to sit with them. Foreseeing an opportunity to learn about traditional Seneca games, I suggested that the committee schedule a slate of native games, an idea which they greeted with enthusiasm and for which I would need help writing publicity for the forthcoming events. Together we produced a series of newspaper columns describing the upcoming games one or two at a time, which the publisher of the Akron weekly printed, also running off reprints sufficient to cover a list of local newspapers in western New York. We even had an event for reservation dogs—an eating contest, proposed by Chief Henan Scrogg, who said that we had provided for everyone else, so why not the dogs? I inadvertently ran it as a "dog eating contest." A crowd of over a thousand people showed up, including western New York's U.S. senator and a member of the House of Representatives. As one local leader predicted, any troubles that my activities had generated vanished.

I had neglected what Jesse Cornplanter called "the salad-eating Indians of Bloomingrove Road"—in short, the progressive element in the community, people who adhered to 4-H and supported the Christian churches. They had complained that I spent too much time "down below," in the Longhouse neighborhood. A Seneca woman who had attended Cornell pointed out the need for a library. We coopted the staff of the Grosvenor Library of Buffalo (now combined with the Erie County Public Library) to visit the reservation, advise on how to organize and maintain the library, and suggest ways to procure duplicate books from other sources. The library thrived for several years until it went up in smoke one night in a mysterious fire, along with the Indian Arts project.

Arthur C. Parker was the genius who thought up the Indian Arts project, which was entirely a Rochester Museum affair; it employed Tonawanda people of all persuasions to re-create objects of their traditional culture in wood, bone, hide, and native textiles. I found the activity fascinating and visited the project daily. Morale was high, and it was fun to hear the repartee that went on in Seneca and reservation English. Bob Tahamont and Cephas Hill, with whom I developed a long friendship, shared supervision.

My sole contribution to the project was to visit, together with Cephas, other regional museums holding Seneca collections, photograph related objects, and supply prints to the artisans. Then as later, Seneca masks and carving preoccupied me (Fenton, Research Report, 1958).

Ernest Smith, the Seneca painter whom the project made famous, went on to produce hundreds of oils and watercolors now in the Rochester Museum collections. Early on he benefited from lessons by Roy M. Mason, whom I introduced to the reservation on a Sunday. The Masons lived in nearby Batavia, where I met them with my fiancée. Years later, with Jeannette Collamer, a student of mine at Albany, I arranged to bring Ernie to Rochester and review his oeuvre on tape.

Hanover Spring, having made his career in the U.S. Navy, returned to the reservation with his bride to find the oil lamps of his boyhood still the sole means of illumination. He set about bringing electric light and power to the reservation and enlisted my help. Together we persuaded the traditional council to grant an easement to Niagara Mohawk in exchange for free electricity in the Longhouse, and despite some questions from the Indian Service in Washington at my not insisting that the power company pay for the easement, the project went through as we planned it.

I make no claim to the community house that was built during my tenure at Tonawanda. It was solely the project of an energetic clergyman's wife from Penn Yan, New York, who convinced herself and some Indians that she was the reincarnation of Mary Jemison, the White Woman of the Genesee, whose captivity narrative has gone to so many editions and reprintings. I did persuade the Akron town fathers to run a water line out to the reservation to supply the needs of the building.

In my second year at Tonawanda, enough money from Field Day collections had reached the Longhouse treasurer to purchase shingles for reroofing the Longhouse. Fortunately, this bit of opulence coincided with the establishment of the National Youth Administration (NYA), for which Louis Bruce, a Sioux-Mohawk educated at Syracuse University, directed programs for the New York Indians. Louis came to Tonawanda looking for activities to employ high-school dropouts. I suggested that we turn two abandoned reservation schools into handball courts where I would teach the lads the game and that we employ another gang to shingle the Longhouse under the direction of one of the chiefs. Henan Scrogg, having worked in construction and being then unemployed, was the logical choice to supervise the work, but I had a hard time persuading him to take the job pro bono, since the NYA provided no funds for supervision. Reluctantly, as a Longhouse officer, he oversaw the work, directing the youths to cut saplings, peel bark, and erect scaffolding. He taught them how to snap a chalk line and replace rotted roof boards and just where to nail the shingles. These were all worthwhile skills to learn. The job got done and the results satisfied most everyone (Fenton and Hill 1935). Louis Bruce later became commissioner of Indian affairs.

By the winter of 1936–37, I sensed that I was going nowhere in the Indian Service and that I had best get busy, write a dissertation, and look for a job teaching in a college or university. In Sapir's famous seminar on "culture and personality," he had set us to devising a situation in which individual behavior had shaped the course of a cultural activity. The Seneca Eagle Dance, which I had first observed at Coldspring and had since observed at Tonawanda, in which the presence or absence of individuals affected the course of ritual, was tailor-made to Sapir's topic. I decided to make a dissertation out of my observations, seek comparative data in neighboring Iroquois communities, search for the dance's ancestry among the Senecas, and map related forms of ritual in North America. As I began to write up my notes, I shared chapters with the savants of the Salt Creek Singers, who became in effect my resident dissertation committee. They caught errors with a concern that I get it right. For ethnographic comparisons I used the libraries of Buffalo. I managed to file the dissertation by the May 15 deadline and went down to New Haven to defend it. When I returned from the defense to the reservation and reported to my Seneca advisors, they asked me to describe the event at Yale and recount how the defense went. Years later, the thesis became a monograph on the Eagle Dance's roots in the Calumet Dance (Fenton 1953).

Marriage to Olive

In late May 1934—while I was still a graduate student, just beginning my second summer of fieldwork and boarding with Henry, Sherman, and Clara Redeye—I acquired a 1926 Packard roadster by paying the overdue storage at Nash's warehouse in Westport. I drove it to Salamanca on the Allegany Reservation of the Seneca Nation. Betimes, I sought the company of old friends. Charles Kammire and his wife, Alene, introduced me to Olive Ortwine, and we all went dancing at the Dudley Hotel. Olive was a beautiful creature, and we got on well together. She had graduated from Syracuse University, which she had attended through the beneficence of an uncle, Harry Vibbard, professor of music, who, having no children of his own, asked the chancellor to provide a scholarship for his niece. Having majored in English, she became a teacher at the upper-high-school level, just then in Oakville, New York, near Batavia and the Tonawanda Senecas. The Redeyes used to tease me for going up to Salamanca evenings and returning downriver late when it was foggy; mist would fill the Allegheny Oxbow. One day Clara asked me, "You aren't going to marry that white girl, are you? We thought you would marry some movie star." By late summer, having picnicked together, swum in the state park, and visited old Cattaraugus County cemeteries, we were (or at least I was) deeply in love.

I had also run low on funds. Olive and I agreed that if I would drive her to Oakfield for the opening of school, she would gas up the Packard. I had some queries to answer for the Indian Service at Tonawanda, and Oakfield was near the reservation. I sensed then that I would return, as indeed I did, in the employ of the Indian Service itself. Olive was a big component in my later choice of an official station at Akron, some fourteen miles west of Oakfield. I returned home to Westport with some reluctance.

My later trips to Oakfield amused the Senecas and added to my list of Seneca place-names. Skenda:di, or, properly, Skayendadi, "Beyond the meadows, over the fields," was an apt name for the area east of the reservation. The term became a source of amusement whenever I appeared at Tonawanda. Olive found me a German tutor in Homer Harvey, MD, of Batavia, a Renaissance type who made violins of orchestra quality and had built his own equatorial telescope. Together, Homer and I read Frederici's monograph *Scalping and Similar Forms of Warfare in America* to prepare me for passing the German requirement for the PhD at Yale. Homer had put himself through the medical program at Syracuse by teaching German to undergraduates, and he was an excellent teacher.

Through Olive's connections in Batavia we met and spent many pleasant hours with Lena and Roy Mason, the painter, who had connections with my father in art circles. Indeed, when Olive and I decided to marry, the Masons supported us at the Episcopal church in Batavia on April 4, 1936, and hosted the celebration afterward.

Not to be outdone by a wedding in a Christian church put on by white people, the Tonawanda Longhouse community decided to celebrate our union in their own way. The Seneca matrons sponsored a great social dance at the Longhouse, draped my bride in yards of annuity goods, and prompted Chief Henan Scrogg as speaker. He held forth on our projected wedding journey south to Washington and Virginia, saying there was no term in the Seneca language for "honeymoon," but if there were, it must be *honey-gahkwa*. Anyway, they expected me to give a full account of our journey on our return, leaving out none of the details.

In Washington we called on Matt Stirling, director of the Bureau of American Ethnology, whom I had met on the Plains several summers previously, in the original "brownstone castle" of the Smithsonian Institution. Somehow we ended up in an office that I was later to occupy, where Frank Speck with a party of students and Truman Michelson were discussing the fine points of Algonquian verbs. It was a terrible ordeal for Olive. Dinner at the home of the Stirlings was certainly less painful.

Next day we departed Washington for the Valley of Virginia to visit Charlottesville, Monticello, and Jefferson's university. Afterward, Olive returned to her teaching and I to the reservation, where I reported on our journey and accepted the teasing of resident wags.[4]

6. 244 State Street East, Westport, Connecticut.

7. Bill at Yale commencement, 1937.

8. John and Anna Fenton, proud parents, 1937.

THREE

From Teaching to the Bureau
of American Ethnology

Having defended my dissertation in May 1937, I returned
to New Haven for commencement to accept the PhD.
Meanwhile, I had been angling for an academic job. At some conference, Edward Sapir met Laurens Seelye, fresh from American
University at Beirut and newly appointed president of St. Lawrence
University (SLU) in Canton, New York. Seeleye was recruiting new
blood to stimulate an established faculty and bring new ideas to
undergraduates. I was one of four who became known as Seelye's
imports. Some townies had less kindly names for us.

I was the first anthropologist to teach at SLU, and it was my
first teaching experience. I landed in the sociology department
under Herb Bloch, who was supportive in every way. He had taught
an introductory course in anthropology the previous year from
Ralph Linton's *The Study of Man*, which he recommended. I was
also assigned two sections of introductory sociology, my major at
Dartmouth. I managed to keep a chapter ahead of the students.

Second semester we had more fun. Having Ernest Benedict, a
native Mohawk from Cornwall Island, in class enabled the other
students to be exposed to an Iroquoian language. Clarence Gaines,
a respected senior professor of English, sat in on the class and
encouraged me. We also illustrated classificatory systems of kinship,

which Afif Tannous, whom Seelye had brought from Lebanon, recognized as similar to his own. Tannous completed the doctorate at Cornell and went on to a distinguished career in the State Department. We met again in Washington.

The college librarians, Miss Dowd and Andy Peters, met our needs by ordering every book I asked for to fill deficiencies in their holdings. I matched teams of students with cultures and sent them to read and report. The sanction to go to the library stacks was somehow appealing to teams of mixed gender.

The cultures of Melanesia became class favorites: Bronislaw Malinowski's *Argonauts of the Western Pacific* and Reo Fortune's then recent *Sorcerers of Dobu*, which even the college president's younger teenage daughter read and reported on in Canton High School, creating a stir in the Canton community. She must have picked up the book at home where her elder sister, who was in my class, had dropped it.

Olive and I, with Betsey, our first child—born in Salamanca on July 4, 1937—found shelter in the home of Lucia Heaton, MD, a pioneer woman physician in the north country and an erstwhile trustee of the college. Dr. Heaton occupied rooms on the second floor, took meals with us, advised me on events transpiring on campus, and went south to live with a nephew during the winter months. Her age mates, who had not been carried off by children's diseases and had survived the cold winters of the north country, came to call afternoons—interrupting Olive's nap—stashed their canes in the hallway, and climbed the stairs to Heaton's quarters. They also populated the Ladies Literary Society, which met in the Canton Public Library. Inevitably, new faculty were summoned to speak.

My turn came too soon. That afternoon I confronted row upon row of ladies dressed in black or dark shades of fabric that set off sorority pins, the odd Phi Beta Kappa key, or other honors. One dear woman held an ear trumpet. I had scarcely begun to speak when she turned to the person seated next to her and remarked in a tone that only the deaf can muster: "I can't hear a thing; is it any good?" I managed to finish and depart as quickly as possible.

One winter afternoon a group of students led by Anders Lunde called at the house, where I was preparing for classes. They had heard that I had coached recreational skiing at Dartmouth. Would I join them in starting a ski program at Canton? Having neither skis, poles, nor boots, I demurred, saying that teaching was my first responsibility. They were not to be put off by academic concerns. The athletics department would outfit me (no mention of compensation). Would I come look at the hill they had found? I went. Within a month the whole community was on skis.

The students not only wanted to ski, they wanted to compete. There was a similar group in nearby Potsdam, guided by Fred Sisson, also a Dartmouth alumnus. We met one afternoon on their hill, and I laid out a slalom course. One of our lads remarked, "That is a nice course. Now let us see you run it." I ran the course and climbed back up. The same young man congratulated me and said, "Professor, you may be a lousy lecturer, but you are a great ski coach." Within a year the students were beyond me, and I persuaded Otto Schniebbs, who was then in Lake Placid, to take over the program before I left for Washington.

Of Seelye's four, I alone made assistant professor. The Committee on Promotion and Tenure included a member of the athletic department who owed me something.

The summer after my first year of teaching at St. Lawrence injected a botanical twist into my research with the Senecas. In previous years of work among them, I had submitted ethnobotanical plant specimens for identification to Robert Gordon, the resident botanist at the Allegany School of Natural History, a biological field station operated by the Buffalo Museum of Science in the Allegany State Park. Dr. Gordon had advised me on field-collecting techniques and preparing herbarium specimens. In conversation, we developed the idea of my running a field school in ethnology among the Senecas under the aegis of St. Lawrence University; the University at Buffalo, with whom the station was affiliated; and the Buffalo Museum of Science. Word went out, and the response was gratifying. Four students enrolled: Ralph Lewis, University of Rochester, afterward with the Museum Division of the National Park Service; Marjorie Lismer, Toronto and Columbia; Ann Schafer, Pennsylvania; and Rose Bleimeyer, biology teacher at Richmond Hills High School, New York City. My Seneca friends could not have been more cooperative. Clara Redeye took two young women under her wing and helped them get started. Ralph Lewis helped me collect medicinals and prepare plants for the herbarium, which Rose Bleimeyer kept in order. I gave two illustrated lectures at the Allegany School of Natural History, which our Seneca friends attended, and we held a great social dance there that everyone enjoyed. Rapport with the Senecas was never higher.

At the end of session I stayed on to work with Chauncey Johnny John on the Little Water Society and its relation to *i:ʔdo:s*, the subject of a recent monograph (Fenton, *Little Water*, 2002). Nevertheless, Olive and I planned to be in Canton for the opening of the college year. We had arranged to rent the house of professor of history Albert Corey, who would be away that year to complete the PhD at Clark University. At the end of August I received a phone call from the president of Lawrence College in Appleton, Wisconsin, inviting me to teach there. While thinking about such a move, a telegram from Matthew Stirling reached me at John Holt's store in Quaker Bridge, offering me the post previously held by J. N. B. Hewitt—who had recently died—at the Bureau of American Ethnology (BAE). Unbeknownst to me, Jesse Cornplanter, my first contact and principal collaborator at Tonawanda and an inveterate letter writer, had touted my capabilities to Hewitt at the BAE, and Hewitt had shown the letter to Stirling, the bureau's director.[1] Stirling was impressed because, he later told me, Indians usually complained about anthropologists. The position carried the rank of assistant anthropologist, with an annual salary of $3,200, a third higher than the salary of an assistant professor at St. Lawrence. When could I report?

Here was an opportunity to devote full time to Iroquoian studies. But I felt obliged to return to St. Lawrence for a semester, until the college could find a replacement for me. First off, I notified Albert Corey, whose house we had rented, so that he could make other arrangements. Second, I planned to notify President Seelye—but before I could reach his secretary for an appointment and before I returned to Canton, Corey had gone to see Seelye, who blew up at the news. "Why come back at all?" he stormed. By the time I met him face to face, President Seelye, whom I liked, had cooled off. We found temporary quarters for the semester. Olive, who was quite pregnant, stayed in Salamanca until after the Christmas break, and I returned to finish the semester.

That fall I taught general anthropology using Franz Boas's book of that title as a text. The book was quite beyond the average student, although two young men built working-model traps from drawings in the chapter on material culture. I displayed them on the lab table of the lecture hall where we met, and before each meeting someone would trip the deadfall with a pencil in a ritual act of continuity. On the day of the final, I boarded the train for Syracuse, managed to scan the bluebooks en route, recorded the grades on the bursar's sheet, and posted them in the first mailbox. Only one student failed.

Olive was full term when my train reached Salamanca. Nevertheless, she vowed to accompany me next morning to the "doings" downriver at Coldspring Longhouse. Bundled in her long raccoon coat, she reminded me of the "Bigheads" who go from house to house announcing the Midwinter Festival. We arrived at the Longhouse in good order, parked the car, and entered the doors sanctioned by long usage for our respective sexes. Armed with Ralph Linton's concepts of "status, role, and participation," I revisited the Midwinter ceremonies with a fresh perspective, instead of simply noting clan and moiety reciprocity. It was amazing how few people carried the ceremony. For her part, Olive was greeted by the matrons and smothered with advice. "Don't hesitate in doorways or you'll have a slow delivery," and so forth. As the weekend approached, and knowing that I should be in Washington to report for work the following week, Olive presented me with a son on February 4, 1939, whom we named John William II, after my father. I stayed by until our physician assured me that mother and child were both fine before I departed for Washington. Ralph and Dorothy Lewis, whom we had met in the summer of 1938, put me up until I could find an apartment. They took me to a cocktail party and introduced me to Ken Disher, who offered me his furnished apartment in Colonial Village in Arlington, which we eventually rented when the Dishers were transferred to Allegany State Park.

Bureau of American Ethnology (1939–1951)

The director and staff of the Bureau of American Ethnology welcomed me as ethnologist on February 6, 1939. I was expected to continue my ethnological studies among Iroquois groups in New York and Canada with a view to defining and cleaning up some ethnological problems in the northeastern area remaining from the research of previous scholars, particularly J. N. B. Hewitt, who had left a score of unpublished works in manuscript. Hewitt had been a perfectionist and a skilled transcriber of texts, but his vast field material had not been published. It took me several years to get a command of the Hewitt Six Nations ceremonial and text notes. I hoped to get some of my own work in print, too.

Matt Stirling assigned me to an office on the second floor of the Smithsonian Institution building, directly over the main entrance and adjacent to the connecting workroom and office of Henry B. Collins, gentleman of Mississippi and Arctic archaeologist, who became my trusted friend and colleague. The previous occupant of my digs, Truman Michelson, Algonquianist and linguist, had filled the cupboards with reprints of notes on the Fox language and culture, which cascaded to the floor when I opened the first paneled door to find space for some books.

John R. Swanton and David I. Bushnell Jr. were the first formal visitors to call and welcome me. Swanton, an early PhD in anthropology from Harvard and the first university-trained member of the BAE staff, was then the reigning authority on southeastern ethnology and linguistics. I had met him previously; he knew my work, and I regarded his research as a model. Bushnell, an independently wealthy scholar, also of Harvard, had run down Native American collections in France and Italy. On leaving, Swanton expressed the hope that I would publish, unlike my predecessor Hewitt, who in his later years had slacked off and left so much in manuscript.

On the heels of my first visitors, the linguist John Peabody Harrington bounced in to announce that we were going to lunch over at the Interior Department cafeteria, some distance down the Mall toward the Lincoln Memorial. Before we left he offered some quick advice: Michelson's Underwood typewriter was obviously inadequate for Iroquoian; I should request a replacement with an additional row of keys to accommodate diacriticals—glottal stop, iota subscript for nasal vowels, and so forth. Second, I should learn Spanish in order to work in Latin America, the current rage, and he would teach me. This was a bit much for one who had come to pursue Iroquoian studies.

J. P. Harrington was a great walker with a long stride. I was then in fair shape and managed to keep up, although I was wearing a double-breasted Ulster that I had brought from the north country. By the time we reached Interior I had worked up a sweat. J. P. had promised that we would meet some Indians. As we sat at lunch, I sensed that a young woman was approaching our table. It was Dorothea Seelye, daughter of President Laurens Seelye at

St. Lawrence and my recent student. J. P. and I stood to greet her, and I introduced J. P. to her, but as she and I talked, I noted that J. P. took an uneaten piece of fish from his plate, wrapped it in a napkin, secured it with rubber bands, and stuffed it in a jacket pocket. Dorothea, having grown up in Beirut and being used to what Americans might consider odd behaviors, never batted an eye.

Harrington and I walked back to the Smithsonian. As we passed the Freer Gallery, J. P. remarked that we would enter the SI building by the rear basement door, from the blind side, where Anthony Wilding, chief clerk of the BAE, could not observe us returning late from lunch. This was only one of J. P.'s eccentricities.

He also had a way of disappearing, telling no one where he was going and sending postcards as he departed without revealing his destination. Once when we all thought he was in Alaska, he turned up in Mexico. His friends knew this when we all received embossed leather briefcases—an Aztec calendar stone and feathered serpent on the front, our initials on the back. (Mine has served me all these years and is now badly worn.) All of this secretive behavior drove the Smithsonian apparatchiks to distraction. Nick Dorsey, treasurer of SI, who had a sense of humor, once asked me, "Where is Harrington just now?"—and pointed to a bundle of U.S. Treasury paychecks stuck to the safe by a magnetic clip.

Julian Steward descended on me a day of so later with his own agenda. He wanted to hear about Sapir's by then famous seminar on culture and personality, which I had attended the second year it ran. Having been reared in the culture-as-superorganic school of A. L. Kroeber at Berkeley, Steward remained skeptical, despite my efforts to explain what Sapir was getting at. What Steward really wanted to hear was a commitment from me to drop everything else and write an overview of the northeast for a festschrift he would edit on "historical anthropology in North America" in honor of John Swanton's fortieth year at SI. Torn between commitments that I had brought with me and Steward's request, I went to see Matt Stirling to learn how I should respond to Steward's request. Stirling, having listened to Steward's proposal without committing himself one way or the other, suggested that I proceed with my own research commitments and take up Steward's proposal as time permitted. Caught between a permissive director and an aggressive colleague who perceived a power vacuum and moved into it, I wrote up my notes on the recent Seneca Midwinter Festival.

In homage to Edward Sapir, who died the week I joined the Bureau, that spring I wrote a monograph on Iroquois suicide from cases I had collected in 1935 at a suggestion made in his seminar (Fenton, "Iroquois Suicide," 1941). I found parallel cases in seventeenth-century sources available in the BAE library. In this study I employed, for the first time, an approach that came to be called "upstreaming," by which I demonstrated the persistence of a culture pattern over time. In later years I found additional cases to bridge a gap in the eighteenth century (Fenton 1986). Lewis Henry Morgan had preceded my residence at Tonawanda in the mid-1930s by ninety years. In 1936 I had contrasted his account of the Longhouse ceremonies with my own account, which I published together with "Iroquois Suicide" as another example of persistence and change during a century (Fenton, "Tonawanda Longhouse Ceremonies," 1941).

Within the first year of my tenure at the BAE, Aleš Hrdlička, the Smithsonian's famous physical anthropologist, published a report in the *Smithsonian Miscellaneous Collections* on a half-dozen skulls from sites in eastern North America, all having missing incisors, which he interpreted as "ritual tooth ablation." Nowhere in the literature on eastern North America that I knew of was any such ritual reported. Not wishing to stick my neck out, I remained silent until one day, T. Dale Stewart, MD, the master's assistant and a colleague, asked me as we were riding to work what I thought of the paper. Without thinking of consequences, but from personal observation of middle-aged Iroquois men, I said, "The skulls are most likely those of former lacrosse players"—victims of cross-checking to the head, now illegal in the sport.

Within a few days, returning from lunch, I met Hrdlička and two head curators, of geology and biology, respectively. This trio, known to their younger colleagues as "the three bastards" from a pun on one of their names, were walking near the Constitution Avenue entrance to the natural history museum. Hrdlička stepped forward and demanded, "You are Fenton: What is this nonsense about lacrosse players and missing incisors?" I replied that I had resided among the Tonawanda Band of Senecas recently for two and a half years and had observed that middle-aged men frequently had one or all of their incisors missing from years at lacrosse. On Hrdlička's insistence for evidence, I wrote to Nick Baily, a lacrosse manager, and asked him to make a headcount among his players and their living antecedents. Nick produced a detailed report, which I sent to Hrdlička. I stopped by the physical anthropology office one day after lunch with Dale Stewart. Presently Hrdlička joined us, the Bailey count in hand, which he refused to accept as supporting my view. On top of it, he remarked, "You know, Fenton, you are getting fat!" I was aware of my gaining weight. My first controversy at SI thus ended on a note of dismissal. Hrdlička's article quietly disappeared into the periodical section of the library stacks, without further challenge.

Soon after arriving at SI, I had moved into Ken Disher's furnished apartment in Arlington, where Olive and the two little ones joined me in March. Apartment living was a new experience for all of us. Olive was used to stepping outside on green grass and hanging a wash on the clothesline. She regarded waiting in turn to use the washer and dryer in the basement as an abomination. Regulations demanded that we store the baby carriage in the basement, but we soon learned the place was infested by rats that chewed any fabric. One winter morning when a few inches of powder snow paralyzed suburban Virginia, I put on my St. Lawrence skis and enjoyed a lovely run down sloping lawns into a ravine—to the delight of neighbors but to the horror of the management. Olive and I were just not suited to apartment living.

At cherry blossom time, my father came down from New York bringing a blue velvet dress from Best's for Betsey and to see his namesake, John. He visited the Smithsonian, met my colleagues, and toured the spots, including the National Zoo, our favorite place just then. Father had recovered from a small stroke several years earlier; a massive stroke would carry him off the following autumn. Mother and my sister, Frances, joined us later. By this time our own furniture arrived from Salamanca, and we had a proper lease for a year. Olive liked to entertain and was a great cook. At St. Lawrence, when friends came to call, one served tea—but we soon learned that in Washington some colleagues and their spouses expected a drink.

I recall one dinner party when Father John M. Cooper of Catholic University, his colleague Regina Flannery, and her husband, the theoretical physicist Karl Hertzfeld, were our guests. Father Cooper and Regina had visited Olive and me in the field at Tonawanda just after we were married and living at Akron, New York. Cooper had sought comparative data on Seneca traps and snares, which he published as an appendix to his monograph on the Cree of James Bay. On this evening, we had little to drink but enjoyed great conversation.

Olive and I commenced looking for a house that we could afford, a place that we could rent summers when I was in the field. Just then three-bedroom houses in the District and nearby Maryland were priced at ten thousand dollars, slightly less in suburban Virginia but beyond our means. Building seemed out of the question.

Julian Steward had a bright idea. Taking a page from the Chicago sociologists, he drew concentric circles around SI on a map at one-mile intervals, out to a ten-mile radius. The largest piece of undeveloped land within that circle was situated at Langley in Virginia, between the Potomac at Great Falls and the road to Leesburg, where the Macall family had surveyed and subdivided Turkey Run into building sites of an acre or more, just ten miles from the Smithsonian. Julian shared his findings with his younger colleagues and urged us to join him in buying lots. I went out to see Buzz Macall, who escorted me on a guided tour of building sites priced at $1,000 per acre. Turkey Run, a small branch of the Potomac, drained a forest of magnificent trees—native tulip poplars, red oaks, and scattered hickories. I chose an acre lot on high ground, well-drained front and back, with access to the road leading to the Lee highway, and took an option. My mother let me have an advance from my father's estate, and we were in business.

Several of us at SI carried our paychecks to the Washington Loan and Trust, a walk up Tenth Street from Constitution Avenue at F Street. Naturally, I went there when seeking a mortgage. The officer who received me listened and then asked, "Is Turkey Run paved? Are there curbs and gutters? What about sewers and water? Until such utilities are available, the bank is not prepared to invest in your property." The same officer would sing a different tune years later.

But I am way ahead of the story and shall have to backtrack.

Late afternoons at the Smithsonian I used to drop in on John Swanton who was then working on the De Soto expedition. He was interested in my research, and he read and commented on my work in progress. A widower with two sons, he accepted our invitations to come out to supper at Turkey Run, family style, which he enjoyed. He read my dissertation and made suggestions. John said, "Publish it; when critics come out of the woodwork you will have another publication."

Fieldwork 1939–1943

In early July 1939 we packed up and removed to Salamanca, New York, so that I could resume ethnobotanical studies among the Iroquois of western New York and Canada. Because I planned to compare Seneca plant uses at several sites and wanted to obviate the problem of finding reservation lodgings, we had purchased an umbrella tent, three cots, a gasoline stove, and cooking utensils. Olive and I tried out the gear in a long weekend at Cornplanter Grant, although my Seneca friends, whose ancestors had often slept on the ground, were horrified and warned us about snakes. None bothered us. My sister, Frances, an honors graduate in botany at Connecticut College, joined us to curate the herbarium specimens, and we headed for Akwesasne (then St. Regis). There we set up camp at Raquette Point on the property of Noah La France, who proved an excellent source on Mohawk ethnobotany. The women cooked some excellent meals on the camp stove, and we were lulled to sleep by the wind off the St. Lawrence. Noah told me that his father, a noted voyageur on the river, had made the long journey to the Rockies for one of the Montreal fur companies. Altogether we enjoyed our week at Raquette Point.

The Longhouse movement was just starting at St. Regis that summer. Its few adherents had coopted a building as a provisional Longhouse, where we were admitted. It was a poor show in contrast to what I was accustomed to among the Senecas. But I did meet Alex Clute, a blind preacher of the Handsome Lake doctrine from Tonawanda, who was instructing the Mohawks in Longhouse ways. He complained to me of his difficulties: "They don't know how to sing, they can't dance, and they are poor speakers." Just now it is hard to imagine that the Longhouse movement at Akwesasne may be little more than sixty years old.

There were no accommodations for camping at Caughnawaga, so we rented a house for one night until we found a campground over the river at LaChine. By this time, Olive and Frances were disenchanted with the camping routine and more interested in the amenities of Montreal. However, in Katie Dybeau, who had served the ethnobotanist F. W. Waugh, I found a gem of an informant on Mohawk medical botany. She immediately recognized the "suicide root" of the Senecas, and the Mohawk cognate by which she knew it preserved much of the Huron form as spelled out in the *Jesuit Relations*[2]—which enabled me to identify the plant for certain as water hemlock *(Cicuta maculata)* and not May apple *(Podophyllum peltatum)* as the editors of the Thwaites edition of the *Relations* thought. Katie, also an active midwife, described for me the whole native birthing process, including cases of breach delivery in which she had participated.

Caughnawaga held a second interest for me. Some two centuries earlier, Father J. F. Lafitau had discovered the North American species of ginseng growing beside a house there and communicated his finding to a scientific journal in Paris, which set off a search for the plant in northeastern America to satisfy the oriental market, which threatened to exterminate the species. Moreover, Lafitau, a perceptive observer of Iroquois life in the village, left an excellent description of Iroquois social and political organization, anticipating Lewis Henry Morgan by a century. The resident priest at Caughnawaga showed us the desk where Lafitau had written, the baptismal records of Lafitau's day, and the church where he said mass. That year Elizabeth Moore and I had begun the translation and editing of Lafitau's great comparative work, which would occupy us off and on during the next thirty-five years (Fenton and Moore, *Customs*, 1974, 1977). The year after the Champlain Society of Toronto brought out our work, the town and the reigning Jesuit of the province invited me to return and address the community.

On the west side of the island of Montreal we touched briefly at Oka, also called Lake of Two Mountains, but properly Kanesatake, "At the side of the mountain" in Mohawk. Finding nothing of interest there, we drove east to Quebec City and out to Lorette, where the Sioui sisters entertained us, although none of them spoke Huron. Their father knew a few native medicinals.

Ottawa held a sufficiency of fieldwork and sightseeing: I examined the file of ethnobotanical photographs from Waugh's work at the National Museum of Canada while Olive and Frances did the town. Diamond Jenness, always a genial host, invited us to come out to his summer place on the Gatineau, where Mrs. Jenness, Edward Sapir's former secretary, told us how she had taken chapters of Sapir's classic *Language* from dictation. The memory of Sapir's genius had lingered in Ottawa for many years after he departed for Chicago.

On our return to Salamanca, where we had left our babies with Olive's mother, Frances returned to Westport and to our mother, who still resided in our State Street house. Olive and I decided to take Betsey, who had just celebrated her second birthday, with us to Brantford, Ontario, and the Six Nations Reserve on Grand River. We called at the Indian Service office, where Hilton Hill, the chief clerk and J. N. B. Hewitt's old friend, introduced us to Colonel Randle, the superintendent, and invited us to camp at the back of his place at Chiefswood. He also arranged for Simeon Gibson to work with me. Olive and Betsey proved favorites of Hilton's wife and daughter and enjoyed the amenities of inside plumbing. We slept soundly in a grove beside the Grand River, although once we were awakened by a fierce visitation of the Thunders, and another time Betsey disappeared from her cot and turned up beneath it, sleeping soundly.

Simeon rowed to Chiefswood daily in a homemade craft that barely qualified as a rowboat. On several days his sister Jemima, a Cayuga clan mother, joined him, for she knew a lot about medicines. Jemima, having known Hewitt, had an agenda of her own that would involve me, as I would discover later. Jemima was incisive and spoke rapidly, whether in her native Cayuga or in English. She did know her herbals and shrubs for emetics. With Simeon's help we reviewed Waugh's notes and collected medicinal plants near our campsite. I photographed Jemima scraping bark for emetics, and we added it to the herbarium, which numbered about one hundred specimens at summer's end. It largely duplicated specimens previously collected among the Senecas. I found interesting similarities in plant use and native terminology among Seneca, Mohawk, and Cayuga-Onondaga sources living on widely separated reservations, which resemblances may reflect older, basic Iroquois botanical concepts and plant uses. In Simeon Gibson I had found a valuable collaborator for work in following years.

Indeed the next year, 1940, Simeon demonstrated his grasp of native religion by outlining and detailing the entire ceremonial cycle at Onondaga Longhouse, including announcements and prayers. The gas attack that he had suffered in the Great War had spoiled his voice for speaking and singing, but it had not impaired his memory. He urged me to get on with the translation of texts: "There are only myself and my brother Hardy who can explain the meanings of the old words. You can read them, but when we are gone the meanings will be lost" (Fenton, "Simeon Gibson," 1944).

In the winter of 1941 Simeon helped record a large number of songs of the Longhouse repertoire, including the rites of the medicine societies, replacing Alexander Goldenweiser's earlier attempts on wax cylinders, since lost. Simeon suggested an even more ambitions plan and volunteered to help bring it off—that we make a documentary film with soundtrack of the fast-failing condolence ceremony for "raising," or installing, chiefs of the Iroquois League, which fitted my plans but which, sadly, never got done, as we shall see. J. N. B. Hewitt had left all the texts of the ceremony in manuscript with hints about the program that governed their performance. Simeon would explain all that, and I would have to learn it.

Simeon's father, Chief John Arthur Gibson, had dictated two Onondaga versions of the legend "Concerning the League," first to Hewitt around 1900 (some 189 typescript pages) and some twelve years later to Alexander Goldenweiser (529 pages on lined legal pads), both of which lacked English translations. Simeon had sat with his father during the first recitation, and he knew about the second. We decided to take them on one at a time. In the autumn of 1941, with a grant from the American Council of Learned Societies, I went up to Brantford by train and put up at the Belmont Hotel, where Hewitt had stayed. Simeon caught a ride mornings with the mail carrier returning from Ohsweken, and we worked intensively for a month as Royal Canadian Air Force training planes zoomed overhead.

One day we had visitors. Simeon's siblings, Jemima and Hardy, came unannounced to remind me that my predecessor, Mr. Hewitt, had promised to sponsor a condolence ceremony for Hardy in the title of their mother's brother Abram Charles, with whom Hewitt had worked and to requicken Hardy in his Cayuga title and seat in the League council.[3] It would be an expensive undertaking, and they would need funds to buy the beef. I agreed to see what could be done to satisfy Hewitt's pledge.

As the days wore on and the work progressed, I missed my wife and children. We devised a way of communicating with them. Simeon, at day's end, would tell a children's folktale, of which he knew an endless store, which I typed out in a letter to my children. Simeon's tales became their favorites, and I later published them as "Letters to an Ethnologist's Children" (Fenton 1948).

Simeon had urged me to get on with translating the ritual texts that Hewitt had left in their native form, most of which pertained to the Condolence Council, which I had yet to witness and describe. The version of the League origin legend that Hewitt recorded from John Arthur Gibson stopped short of describing the great ceremony for mourning deceased chiefs and raising their successors in office, but Chief Gibson had given a full account of the ceremony in the version of the legend that he dictated to Goldenweiser in 1912.[4] After Pearl Harbor I took a break from war work, went up to Brantford by train, and stayed at Ohsweken, where Simeon and I worked through that section of the Goldenweiser manuscript bearing on the condolence ceremony. His knowledge enabled me to identify its principal parts, fix the order of ceremony, and derive its major concepts.

We had further plans for collaboration, but Death the Faceless struck the reserve on the night of December 10, 1943. Simeon left his home that blustery night and crossed the Grand River in his makeshift craft to buy groceries at Middleport, as was his custom. It is presumed that he drowned during the return trip in a storm that swept the Niagara peninsula that evening (Fenton, "Simeon Gibson," 1944).

In the Brownstone Tower

Winters in the "brownstone tower" I had read the historical literature, located the towns of the several Iroquois bands at successive periods in their history, and outlined the cultural problems arising from their tribal movements and conquests. This study (Fenton, "Problems Arising," 1940), which benefited from Julian Steward's editing,[5] attempted for the Northeast the kind of systematic approach that Swanton had accomplished for the Southeast and appeared in a volume honoring the great scholar. It defined a whole field of study and generated a great deal of later research. The anthropologist Bruce Trigger proclaimed it "the most important piece on the Iroquois up to 1940."

Two other projects hung fire: my early fieldwork on medicinal plants and an abiding interest in the Iroquois False Face Society and its masks. With a background of observations, I had embarked on a systematic study of older masks in museum collections and reviewed my photographs with living carvers. I had outlined a monograph and filed notes in labeled folders. Recalling Professor

Sapir's advice to write summary papers on major projects early on, "for they may be the best thing we have for many years," I welcomed the invitation to staff members to contribute articles as supplements to the *Annual Report of the Smithsonian Institution*. "Masked Medicine Societies of the Iroquois" (Fenton 1941) prompted readers with a wide variety of interests in masks to write to me. Sapir was right: years later, in retirement, I wrote the major book on the subject (Fenton, *False Faces*, 1987).

I summarized my ethnobotanical studies in a second article for the 1941 annual report, entitled "Contacts between Iroquois Herbalism and Colonial Medicine." It appeared just after Pearl Harbor. The piece aroused the National Institutes of Health to copy my herbarium file for possible anticarcinogenic agents, although a member of Congress, during budget hearings, questioned the propriety of publishing such esoteric research when the nation was at war. To be discovered by Congress is the worst thing that can happen to a civil servant. I was called on the carpet by an intimidated assistant secretary and told virtually to get lost. It remained for a graduate student of mine to write the monograph.[6]

FOUR

The War and Postwar Years

I had barely returned to Turkey Run from Six Nations when on a December Sunday, Olive's mother, whom the children had dubbed "Bonner," had a guest from Salamanca who wished to visit Arlington Cemetery. I vividly recall standing near the Lee Mansion when a nearby radio blared the news of Pearl Harbor. As we crossed Memorial Bridge toward the Lincoln Memorial to pick up the bypass to Georgetown, uniformed officers were scurrying toward the temporary buildings that had lined Constitution Avenue since World War I. On Monday we were all wondering just how the national disaster would affect us.

The first reactions at the Smithsonian were passive and then defensive. A general apathy gave way to concern for the collections. Type specimens and rare books from the libraries soon were evacuated and sequestered in the mountains of Virginia, which affected research routine. My colleague Henry Collins and I began to talk. Through contacts with panels at the National Research Council (NRC), we became aware that colleagues in anthropology and geography were being recruited for the intelligence services. There was a demand for scientists and academicians who knew areas where the war was being fought and had photographs, maps, and linguistic skills, and we recognized that the Smithsonian staff included persons with such knowledge and skills. We prepared a memorandum and carried it to the secretary of SI, Charles Greeley Abbott. He did an unprecedented thing: he called a staff meeting of the Smithsonian "brass" and head curators, to whom Collins and I presented the case for participation in the war effort.

Anthropologists commenced to arrive in Washington early in 1942 to take up posts in the new war agencies, and they soon sought out their colleagues at the Smithsonian. With the help of Collins, Steward, and Alfred Métraux, I began to compile a cumulative roster of personnel and the agencies in which the new arrivals were employed. The Anthropological Society of Washington, of which I was then secretary, opened a door for them at its monthly meetings in the U.S. National Museum. Among the first to arrive were Ruth Benedict from Columbia and Clyde Kluckhohn from Harvard.

Secretary Abbott then did a second unprecedented thing. With the advice of Assistant Secretary Alexander Wetmore, the noted ornithologist and director of the U.S. National Museum, he established the Smithsonian War Committee to coordinate the institution's contribution to the war effort. The two of them entrusted its conduct to a safe administrator, Carl Mittman, and named Herbert Friedmann, curator of birds; Webster True, chief of publications; and myself to the committee. I served as secretary. At my suggestion the committee drafted and distributed a questionnaire, first among SI's own personnel, soliciting basic data for what became "a roster of personnel, world travel, and special knowledge available to war agencies at the Smithsonian Institution."

The committee entrusted the compilation of the roster to me. Collins and I designed it after the personnel lists of the Oceania committee of Ethnographic Board at the National Research Council, where we both had served on a parallel committee. By early summer, the Smithsonian roster approached final form.

Word reached us that Carl Guthe was in town trying to revive the moribund Ethnographic Board at the NRC by widening its scope to include geography, then in demand at war agencies, and enlisting William Duncan Strong, formerly of the BAE but then at Columbia, to direct it. I reported this intelligence to Secretary Abbott, with whom I had developed some rapport, recommending that SI with its outreach to the learned world host the project and invite Duncan Strong to return home. Next day I was summoned to the secretary's office and directed to go to New York, extend an invitation to Strong, and return within the day. "Go by coach," Abbott said, "I always do." The Smithsonian would house the project, assign staff to its work, and pay the director's salary.

Within the week, both Guthe and Strong were on the ground surveying the scene, strengthening the tie of NRC to SI and broadening sponsorship to embrace the Social Science Research Council and the intensive language program of the American Council of Learned Societies.

By early summer both Collins and I were detailed to assist the director of the new Ethnogeographic Board. Iroquois studies and Arctic prehistory activities were suspended for the duration. I did take a break, however. At the request of the Pennsylvania Historical Commission, I made a brief field trip to the Cornplanter Grant in northwestern Pennsylvania with Merle Deardorff, of Warren, Pennsylvania, to pursue our common interest in Seneca place-names and related activities such as hunting and fishing along the Allegheny River. Expecting little information from this long missionized community, in contrast with sources in the traditional Coldspring Longhouse community upriver, to my amazement I collected from Willie Gordon, a lifetime Cornplanter resident, an account of the last passenger pigeon hunt of the Senecas (Fenton and Deardorff, "Pigeon Hunts, 1943). The series on place-names ran later in the *Pennsylvania Archaeologist* (Fenton, "Fish Drives," 1942; "Place Names," 1945, 1946).

Back in Washington, I devoted the remainder of the year to projects generated by the Smithsonian War Committee and the Ethnogeographic Board. For nearly a century, "the increase and diffusion of knowledge" had been SI's stated purpose. Doing what the institution did best, the War Committee launched a series of *War Background Studies* by area specialists, first SI staff and later specialists who had come to town. I volunteered to do Australia, but after extensive reading in the scientific and popular literature—without ever setting eyes on the place—I just could not bring myself to write up my notes.

By this time the armed forces and other war agencies had been alerted to the "roster of personnel, world travel, and special knowledge available . . . at the Smithsonian Institution," first compiled by the War Committee. It had expanded to include the learned world within the United States and then evolved into the World

File of Regional Specialists at the Ethnogeographic Board. The file included more than twenty-five hundred names of individuals, their travel experience, and their special knowledge. It had been my idea, and I was charged with responsibility for it. My Yale background included courses on Melanesia under Richard Thurnwald of Berlin and on Polynesia with the noted Maori scholar Sir Peter Buck, both areas of interest to the navy, and I remembered enough navigation from undergraduate astronomy at Dartmouth to converse with naval officers. Moreover, I knew the ethnographic literature on both areas and how to get at it. For example, I recalled that Thurnwald had done fieldwork on the island of Buin near Guadalcanal. His published monograph, *Lieder und Sagen aus Buin* (Songs and tales from Buin), carried a German admiralty map of the island that showed the trails made by the natives. The Office of Naval Intelligence (ONI) passed it along to the Marine Corps.

The file of area and language specialists came into extensive use by various intelligence branches of the armed forces and by related agencies. Using familiar anthropological techniques, I prepared for the photographic division of ONI a series of five studies, together with maps and indices, showing domestic sources of photographs on strategic areas of concern to the navy. I clearly recall walking a second of these studies down the Mall from the old brownstone tower of SI toward the temporary building on Constitution Avenue that housed the photographic division of ONI where in the course of my visit, I had occasion to refer to an earlier study. By then it had been classified and was no longer for my civilian eyes—but it was arranged for me to see the report while an officer with captain's stripes looked over my shoulder to make certain that I copied nothing. He was intrigued to hear how I had assembled the information.

I enjoyed the contacts at ONI, and toward the end of my stint with it, Olive and I hosted a mint julep party for naval officers at Turkey Run. They all came. Walter Muir Whitehill of Salem, Massachusetts historian of the war in the Pacific and later director of the Athenaeum in Boston, graced the party with his handlebar moustache. There was not a sprig of mint left growing in McLean, Virginia, and scarcely a drop of bourbon in Fairfax County when the sun went down that weekend.

Meanwhile, the American Council of Learned Societies (ACLS)

had mobilized the linguists of America, who had converted methods of analysis to methods of teaching. The Intensive Language Teaching Program had achieved remarkable success in meeting the demand for trained interpreters and liaison officers in foreign areas. The Army Specialized Training Program–Foreign Area Language (ASTP–FAL) was in full swing when Mortimer Graves of ACLS approached the Ethnogeographic Board suggesting that we as anthropologists examine the area aspect of the program for the implications this interdisciplinary effort might hold for undergraduate teaching. Presently, the Army Specialized Training Division of the provost marshal's office requested that we survey the ASTP–FAL as well as the Civil Affairs Training (CATS) programs in twenty-five American universities and colleges. I was assigned to conduct the survey along with Elizabeth Bacon, who joined the Ethnogeographic Board staff for that purpose. Between December 1943 and March 1944, Bacon visited twelve institutions, and I covered the other thirteen. ASTP–FAL was for noncommissioned personnel; the CATS programs trained officers as administrators. I wrote up reports promptly for circulation to the heads of programs affected, with copies to Graves at ACLS and for internal discussion. From this experience I learned several lessons about writing: if my reports were favorable, readers commended my prose; if unfavorable or highly critical, the writing was deplored. Bacon and I were soon at odds over emphasis and content. Ultimately Bacon resigned, and several years later I wrote the final report for a committee of the American Council on Education (Fenton, "Area Studies," 1947). It coincided with the end of the Ethnogeographic Board and discharged my final obligation to wartime activities.

The demands of the Ethnogeographic Board slacked off toward the end of 1944, and I found time for Iroquois studies once more. Although SI had shut down scientific publication for the duration of the war, the *Journal of the Washington Academy of Sciences* (JWAS), of which I was now a coeditor, afforded an outlet. I could now welcome other anthropologists who were engaged in war work to submit articles. Thus JWAS carried some important contributions, notably Dimitri Shimkin's analysis of Great Basin mythology; Morris Opler's "Theory of Themes," and my own "The Last Passenger Pigeon Hunts of the Cornplanter Senecas" (with M. H. Deardorff), as well as my first BAE assignment, that of editing J. N. B. Hewitt's "The Requickening Address of the Iroquois

Condolence Council" (Fenton, ed., 1944). I also contributed an obituary of my greatest informant: Simeon Gibson, 1889–1943, to the *American Anthropologist* (Fenton 1944).

The First Lady Addresses the Academy

Early on at the BAE, I joined the Anthropological Society of Washington (ASW), a predecessor and founder of the American Anthropological Association, and attended its monthly meetings in room 43 of the U.S. National Museum. Within a year I became secretary and chairman of the program committee. The society welcomed anthropologists recently come to town in the war effort, who found relief from classified restrictions in the chance to hear and discuss professional matters. They also proved a boon to the program committee, for among them I found an abundance of speakers.

After Pearl Harbor, the army had begun shipping whole regiments to staging areas in New Zealand and Australia, where as guests of our allies they posed something of a burden to the local residents. Some of us wondered how the Yanks were getting on with the Kiwis and Aussies. First Lady Eleanor Roosevelt wondered, too, and decided to go find out for herself. It was a bold adventure flying in wartime in military aircraft of the day, and a long flight even later in jets. Mrs. Roosevelt made the trip out and back safely. She talked with hundreds of "her" boys and listened to their hosts, and the Washington papers ran numerous articles about her adventure.

One afternoon soon after her return, Herbert Krieger, then curator of ethnology at the U.S. National Museum (USNM), phoned to say that his daughter had suggested that the Anthropological Society of Washington should invite Mrs. Roosevelt to share her findings with the society. Would I, as secretary of ASW and chairman of its Program Committee, dare invite her?

Without thinking too much of the consequences, I wrote a letter to the First Lady, told her about ASW and its meetings, and said that we anthropologists would like to hear what she had learned about the impact of our troops on the people of the South Pacific—that no one was better qualified than she to assess how our lads were getting on with their hosts. I addressed the letter to the White House, put it in the outgoing mail, and returned to my research.

One morning I was deep in the BAE library stacks checking references for a monograph prior to publication when I was called to the phone. The White House was calling! Mrs. Roosevelt would like to accept. Could I arrange to meet with her? Knowing that Mrs. Roosevelt frequently walked over to the Cosmos Club, entered by the ladies' entrance, and lunched with a relative, a retired resident clergyman, I suggested we meet at the club of which I was a member. The White House would send a car for me on the appointed day.

When I returned to my office, the phone was ringing steadily. It was Harry Dorsey, administrative assistant to Secretary Abbott, demanding to know why I was calling the White House, which was the prerogative of the secretary of SI. He suggested I come down and explain. (Nick and Harry Dorsey were Maryland boys who had come to the Smithsonian in Secretary Langley's time as messenger boys and worked their way up to the higher clerical ranks; Nick, a genial soul, was treasurer of SI.) When I explained to Harry that I had written the White House on behalf of ASW, on the society's letterhead, he simmered down. The White House had tracked me to SI.

Word that the First Lady would address ASW spread rapidly through the Smithsonian and reached officers of the Washington Academy of Sciences, an umbrella for constituent local scientific societies. Frank Setzler, head curator of anthropology at USNM, phoned to say that the president of the academy would like to broaden the auspices of Mrs. Roosevelt's talk to embrace all of the academy's constituent societies. Would ASW yield?

I had had enough notoriety and was glad to shift the responsibility to a broader context.

The White House called again. This time the Smithsonian switchboard did not panic. Mrs. Roosevelt could not keep our luncheon arrangement, but she would address the academy. The president, Secretary Abbott reported, was teasing the First Lady unmercifully about her ignorance of the peoples of Oceania—saying she didn't know Melanesians from Polynesians—and I was not to tell her. I assured the secretary that it was more important for us to hear what she learned about the impact of her boys on their hosts in New Zealand and Australia.

Meanwhile, the USNM was abuzz with activity. With the academy as host, the lecture was moved to the auditorium, which was being cleaned, inspected by the Secret Service, and the stage set to accommodate Smithsonian hosts, the president of the academy, and the First Lady. The academy issued printed invitations to a lecture by Mrs. Roosevelt on "Civilization in the South Pacific" and mailed them to all members of its constituent societies and their spouses.

Until the night of the lecture, I had not talked to or met with Mrs. Roosevelt. Olive and I joined the queue of our colleagues in the hallway leading to the auditorium, where Mrs. Roosevelt was greeting everyone as they came in. Having identified myself and introduced Olive, we chatted briefly. I thanked her for honoring my invitation and mentioned we were native New Yorkers, of New Rochelle and Salamanca, both of which she knew well.

The lecture went well. Mrs. Roosevelt held her audience, and everyone seemed satisfied. We sat in the audience among friends and colleagues. No mention was made of my role in the affair, although it was not forgotten by the hierarchy of SI.

The Cosmos Club

The Cosmos Club was where the informal business of science in Washington was transacted over lunch, where one might encounter someone with advice on how to approach a problem involving another agency, or where one simply went after work to relax. Paul Oehser, poet, editor, wit, and my lifelong friend, and Matt Stirling, chief of the BAE, sponsored me for membership, and the committee on admissions agreed that I had made significant contributions to ethnology sufficient to warrant election.

Cosmos has a distinguished history. It was founded in 1878 by Maj. J. Wesley Powell, of Civil War and Grand Canyon fame, creator of the BAE and lifetime chief, as well as founder of the U.S. Geological Survey, and a group of other worthies that included the geologist Clarence King and the historian Henry Adams. These men set the tone for what was to follow. From the beginning, "the acquisition and maintenance of a library" ranked high in the club's stated purposes.

As a junior member of the club in 1942, I kept a low profile among my seniors and long-time members, aside from going there for lunch occasionally. It was a nice walk from the SI to Lafayette Square. Paul Oehser, by then secretary of the club, often had business to perform, and he and I would pick up Harald Rehder, mala-cologist at the USNM, and walk up Pennsylvania Avenue, pass the Treasury at Fifteenth Street, and meet Harold Zahnhiser, founder of the Wilderness Society, to make up a table where we ate the thirty-five-cent lunch—a plate of soup, bread, and a beverage—while we discussed matters of mutual interest. When alone, one might sit at one of two long tables—"Cosmos Club Common" or "Cosmos Club Preferred"—where Herbert Putnam, Librarian of Congress Emeritus, presided. There was good conversation whichever table one chose. Nonresident members, there for the war effort and eager to discuss other things, might sit opposite or beside one. I recall such chance encounters once with James Bryant Conant of Harvard and another time with Vanever Bush of MIT. Just then I was reviewing books in my field for New York and Washington newspapers, and I was soon appointed to the library committee.

After the club removed to its present location at 2121 Massachusetts Avenue, I became chairman of the library com-mittee. It was the custom for club authors to deposit copies of their most recent books in the library, where they were put on display for ready access. Some of these works dealt with issues of the day. Sensing that too few members managed to regularly scan this shelf, I thought we should invite the authors themselves to relate the gist of their work in fifteen-minute after-dinner talks to members. The idea of book suppers was one of two bright ideas of my lifetime (the other the Conference on Iroquois Research). I shall let Wilcomb Washburn describe this club innovation in his history of the club.

> One of the most interesting achievements of the Library Committee was the introduction of a series of "Book and Author Suppers" which continue to this day. The first such supper was held on March 23, 1954, attended by a capacity crowd of one hundred. The idea came from William N. Fenton, the new chairman of the Library Committee, who stimulated his committee at its first meeting on February 15 to carry out the scheme in order to increase the appreciation of the Cosmos Club's books and their authors. Dwight Gray of the Library Committee organized the suppers. Dr. Fenton's idea was to ask members to discuss their latest volumes at special Club dinners which would be informal enough to be called suppers. A. Powell Davies, pastor of All Souls

Unitarian Church, the first speaker, discussed his book *The Urge to Persecute* [this was the height of the McCarthy era]. The ground rules for the suppers were laid out in Dwight Gray's notes introducing a later speaker, Winifred Overholser: "A. We are a club of gentlemen. B. Differences of opinions are welcome, nay courted. C. Immunity from the Press [both Walter Lippman and Marquis Childs attended]. D. No sermons from the floor.[1]

By the centennial of the Cosmos Club the Book and Author Suppers had already become a club tradition. Even after I left the BAE and moved to Albany in July 1954, I assumed nonresident membership for a year or so, after which family obligations, with two children in college, called for some retrenchment. I resigned with some regret. To my amazement, I received a letter from Admiral Duval, a senior resident of the club, who had appointed himself watchdog over library acquisitions and had complained that the library committee had recently been favoring the more liberal authors and particular liberal periodicals on our subscription list; if I were in financial straits, he would pay my dues. I was touched. I replied to Admiral Duval, thanked him, and explained that this was a family matter, a priority above the club.

Back among the Iroquois

The quality of the previous sound recordings I had made of Seneca songs had sufficiently impressed the staff of the Library of Congress recording laboratory that they supported a petition I made to the chief of the music division in 1945. I asked to borrow the library's sound truck for fieldwork at the Six Nations Reserve in Canada, and Jerry Wiesner proceeded to instruct me in its use. I had somehow made better use of equipment than some folklorists and had caught the quality of Iroquois singers; I had let them judge by native standards how to balance the percussion of drum and rattles versus their voices by instructing one of them to manage the controls. Jerry recorded his precise operating instructions but protested that I didn't listen. I replied, "I rely on smart Indians."

Following the first Conference on Iroquois Research in 1945, which met, courtesy of Commissioner Charles E. Congdon, in the administration building of Allegany State Park, I drove the sound truck from the Library of Congress to Ohsweken on Six Nations Reserve. There I joined Frank Speck and Ernest and Irene

Dodge of the Peabody Museum at Salem, who went on ahead to Sadie Jamieson's. Elsewhere I have described our memorable joint effort at fieldwork when I cut a disk of Frank and his Delaware collaborator recalling bird names. We also recorded the Dark Dance at the home of Speck's Cayuga colleague Deskaheh, Alex General, later one of my sources on the Condolence Council (Fenton, "Speck's Anthropology," 1990). I helped Ernest Dodge capture some intriguing flute songs, which remain unpublished. Frank Speck was inside while I stayed in the truck managing the controls. He came out eventually and said, "They are bored, let us shut it down." The Dodges and Speck departed, while I stayed on to work out the program of the Condolence Council with Howard Skye and try to persuade the council elders to let me film the ceremony.

Howard advised that I make a formal presentation to the chiefs at their next meeting and that I address them in the Onondaga language. He would tell me what to say, and I would write it phonetically. Using the correct forms would help. This we did. I memorized the opening greeting and the closing forms, which I still recall, and I read the rest.

On the appointed day, armed with my speech and a box of cigars, I waited beside the road that passes Onondaga while the chiefs opened the council. They sent a deputy to take me by the arm, usher me into the Longhouse, and seat me opposite the chiefs. Presently their speaker announced that floor was now open for me to speak. At the formal greeting, "Chiefs, warriors, women, and even the children," their faces brightened. I stumbled through the justification while they listened, and closed with, "That is the sum of my words. That is it."

I then returned to the edge of the road to sit while they deliberated. I could hear the speeches, but not their content. Presently, Alex Nanticoke, a Cayuga chief, came out and sat beside me. I inquired how it was going. It was a tough proposition, and he needed another cigar, and several for other chiefs, which I gave him, and he went back inside. In due course I was ushered back inside the Longhouse and again seated opposite the chiefs.

After a dignified pause, the appointed speaker stood and pronounced the verdict. The chiefs were of one mind that I should not make a movie of the condolence ceremony. Although they trusted me, the film might get out of my hands and be shown in theaters across Canada. The very thought of exploiting their most sacred ceremony offended them. They were holding the ceremony, nevertheless, and they invited me to attend the rehearsal in Onondaga Longhouse so that I could learn the ceremony along with their young men. Then, on the great day of its performance, I would know what to expect. They hoped that I would attend both the rehearsal and the performance.

In a way I was relieved. I had already contracted to buy the beef for the terminal feast. Howard Skye had tutored me on the order of ceremony, and I was now free to observe and listen without the encumbrance of a movie camera, a medium unfamiliar to me. Bob and Marcel Hatt, who were prepared to film with me, graciously accepted the role of observers. I would try to make amends afterward to Paul Fejos and the Viking Fund, who had made it all possible. I described my role in the rehearsal in my monograph on the condolence cane (Fenton 1950) and the great ceremony itself in "An Iroquois Condolence Council for Installing Cayuga Chiefs in 1945" (Fenton 1946). I still regard this as my best piece of fieldwork.

Not only that, but on August 5 of that year—at the very end of the world war, and after having earlier lost our son Harry to cancer—Betsey and John got a new brother, Douglas Bruce.[2]

Northwestern

In 1946 I began serving on a new Committee on International Relations in Anthropology organized by the anthropologist Melville J. Herskovits, of Northwestern University, for the National Research Council of the National Academy of Sciences (NAS).[3] Serving on a committee of the NRC makes one visible in the academic world. One day in the spring of 1947, Mel Herskovits called on me at the Smithsonian and, in the course of conversation, informed me that A. Irving "Pete" Hallowell was returning home from Northwestern to Philadelphia to resume his professorship at the University of Pennsylvania. Would I be interested in replacing him? Aware of my growing interest in the political history of the Iroquois League, he sensed that political anthropology and ethnohistory were fertile fields in our discipline. Meanwhile, would I join Carl Voegelin (Indiana) for the summer session? I agreed to the latter, but removing permanently from Turkey Run to Evanston and abandoning my post at SI would take careful consideration. (I did not yet know that I would not be the first candidate for Pete Hallowell's professorship.)

I went out to Evanston with two things in mind: find a house to rent for the summer session and make the academic rounds for a professorship. The first was easy. Mel had found the house of a colleague going on leave for the year that would accommodate my extended family. The place was an architectural gem, one of a pair side-by-side by Frank Lloyd Wright, which the owner let us have for the summer or for a year at a reasonable rent. Rooms were on different levels at odd angles, so that in going from one room to the next, one took a half-flight of stairs. I thought we would all suffer shin-splints by summer's end. But we all came to enjoy the house.

The academic round was something else. Mel escorted me to the president's office, where on entering we ran into the vice-president of the university, a giant of a man named Stagg, well above six-feet-two, who joined us there, sparing himself and me another interview. (Stagg was about to depart for LA to fill the presidency at USC.) President Franklin Bliss Snyder, erstwhile professor of English literature, seated behind a huge mahogany desk, did not rise to greet us, for he was otherwise occupied and in a bad mood.

We seated ourselves in a semicircle, Mel on my left and Stagg on my right, I in the center. He immediately turned to Herskovits and demanded why Mel had not warned him that he was coming out for Henry Wallace for president. A reporter at the *Chicago Tribune* had called him in the middle of the night asking for comment for a column he was writing citing Northwestern for harboring New Deal liberals. That set the tone for my interview.

Mr. Snyder then turned to a shelf of reference books, pulled down *Who's Who in America*, found my entry and, addressing me for the first time, remarked, "I see you are in here. There was a John Fenton at Beloit College who borrowed five dollars from me and never paid it back." This was too much for me. Although my father of that name had been gone eight years, it all came back to me. I exploded. Without regard to the consequences, I blurted out, "No member of the Fenton family ever heard of Beloit College!" That ended my chances for a professorship at Northwestern University. I did meet with Dean Leland of the graduate school, who was greatly amused by my encounter with President Snyder.

On returning to Washington, I ran into Mortimer Graves of ACLS, my mentor on area studies, at the Cosmos Club, and he asked me about my trip to Evanston. I recounted my encounter with Franklin Snyder. "You should have said no member of your family ever had five dollars. Franklin Snyder is the only man I know who can strut in bed."

The professorship gone with the wind that sweeps into Evanston off the prairie in summer, we Fentons, nevertheless, fulfilled our obligation to Mel Herskovits. We rented our Turkey Run house, packed the car and drove to the windy city to occupy the Frank Lloyd Wright house while I taught two courses. My colleague for the summer, Carl Voegelin of Indiana University, whom I knew from Yale and who had turned down Pete Hallowell's professorship, immediately called on us and stayed for supper. He soon became our frequent guest and a favorite of our children, engaging Betsey or John in games of chess after supper, invariably winning until they finally conspired to beat him.

Returning to the BAE after holding a professorship for a quarter in a major university seemed rather dull. There were no longer funds for research travel such as I had enjoyed at the Ethnogeographic Board, and the title of senior ethnologist seemed pointless unless something happened to increase salary and support. I could still manage two weeks of fieldwork at Allegany Reservation, by now my second home.

Teaching a course in nonstate political institutions that summer at Northwestern, however, had suggested a plan for undertaking a comprehensive political history of the Iroquois League that would employ the findings of ethnology for interpreting the historian's customary sources. I thought this approach might yield new insights into the historical process and afford a time perspective for cultural institutions that either escape the notice of historians or do not interest them. I had made a beginning with the papers of Samuel Kirkland (1748–1808), missionary to the Oneidas; and Arthur Parker had introduced me to the papers of Asher Wright, missionary at Buffalo Creek in the nineteenth century—so I knew that such sources existed.

Paul Wallace, literary historian, put this bee in my bonnet. He had spent days in my office soon after Pearl Harbor when I was preoccupied with the Ethnogeographic Board, examining the translation of Hewitt's text of the turn-of-the-century Gibson version of "Concerning the League," which Simeon Gibson and I had translated the previous autumn. Wallace would soon write his now classic *The White Roots of Peace* (1946), with generous credit. We talked about support for my project, and Paul introduced me to William E. "Billy" Lingelbach, librarian of the American Philosophical Society (APS), who appointed me fellow of the APS Library with money from the Phillips Fund for travel to repositories. Professor Cornelius Osgood of Yale opened doors for me at the Viking Fund (later the Wenner-Gren Foundation for Anthropological Research), which granted funds for further fieldwork related to my project. Overnight, my ability to pursue important research at the Smithsonian had changed. It resembled an episode out of Grimm.

Early on I sought the advice of the noted bibliographer R. W. G. Vail, director of the New York Historical Society, who named repositories containing papers pertinent to my project and suggested a strategy for my visits. He advised tackling the big collections first. I went first to Boston and Salem, Massachusetts, where Ernest Dodge had eased the way for my examining the Timothy Pickering Papers at the Massachusetts Historical Society, the Essex Institute, and the Peabody Museum, of which Dodge became director. On one of my Salem visits, Dodge and I called on Timothy Pickering's descendents, then living in the Pickering House, where a daughter later discovered in the rafters a packet of letters written by Timothy to his wife during the Canandaigua Treaty negotiations of 1794, containing observations on Seneca family life unreported elsewhere. The fifteen folio volumes of mementos relating to western New York that Henry O'Reilly assembled and donated to the New York Historical Society—the background of Timothy Pickering's treaty with the Six Nations—merited repeated trips to New York City, where I also examined the papers of Philip Schuyler at the New York Public Library.

The library fellowship enabled me to canvass large collections such as the Massachusetts Archives in Boston, list items for microfilming, and employ a typist to transcribe the hearts of relevant documents on five-by-eight-inch slips for filing chronologically. Meanwhile, I identified Seth Newhouse as author of several native documents, principally the "Butcher Book," in which he had written several versions of the condolence rituals in Mohawk and in reservation English. Somehow the book had migrated from Six Nations on Grand River to Akwesasne (St. Regis), where Paul Wallace had persuaded Ray Fadden to let him bring it to Philadelphia for study.

Dr. Lingelbach invited me to summarize progress on my search for sources for my projected "Political History of the Six Nations Iroquois" and present it at the autumn meeting of the American Philosophical Society in November 1948. Accordingly, I prepared a twenty-minute paper outlining my approach employing ethnological studies for interpreting historical sources and proceeding against the flow of history, a method I called "upstreaming," with examples. I managed to keep my talk within the time frame measured by an hourglass watched by the presiding chairman. Merle Curti, intellectual historian of Wisconsin, responded favorably and encouraged me to proceed. He made my day.

I stayed by for the afternoon session. Various notables drifted in, including H. L. Mencken of Baltimore and publisher Alfred Knopf of New York, wearing a pink shirt open at the collar and no jacket. The two exchanged loud greetings. Somehow, at the end of the session I found myself coopted by a group dominated by the two notables; we gathered at an upright piano that stood against the wall of the meeting room. I recall that Mencken sat at the keyboard and commenced to play, while Knopf marshaled his audience and later conducted us to dinner at Bookbinders.

During several visits to Hamilton College Library in Clinton, New York, originally a school for the children of Oneida Indians, I became fascinated by missionary Samuel Kirkland's "plan of education," which stemmed from a conviction that Native Americans as humans were educable and which led to the founding of the college. The then librarian of the college, a man named Wilder, invited me to give a public lecture to students and faculty. I selected Kirkland's plan as my topic and delivered the talk in the old college church that Kirkland had built for the Oneidas.

Things seldom work out as planned. Family obligations, other assignments, jobs, and personal health intervened to postpone my writing the political history of the Iroquois until much later in life. Over the years I wrote articles on crucial topics—cosmology, culture patterns, mnemonic systems, and wampum, coupled with observations of the Condolence Council—that in retirement became chapters in *The Great Law and the Longhouse* (Fenton 1998).

Factionalism: The Great Western Trip, 1950

Charles Greeley Abbott having retired, Alexander Wetmore moved up from director of the U.S. National Museum to secretary of the Smithsonian. Save for my interest in passenger pigeons, ornithologist Wetmore took a dim view of my freewheeling activities in wartime and deprecated my passion for Iroquois studies. Favoring large, systematic studies, he remarked that I wrote too many short pieces and published in too many places outside of si. In order to move me toward a broader interest, he appointed me to represent si on the Inter American Committee on Indian Affairs, chaired by the secretary of the interior, Oscar Chapman. Willard Beatty, director of education, and Darcy McNickel, tribal organization, represented the Bureau of Indian Affairs (bia). It was a good committee.

At our May meeting in 1950, Oscar Chapman had something on his mind. The bia's Southwest area director at Albuquerque, New Mexico, had gone up to Taos Pueblo in the interest of making peace between two factions, and it was alleged that the conservative faction had ushered him out of the pueblo. What is more, there were similar problems at Klamath, Oregon, and at Browning, Montana, among the Blackfeet. Someone should look into this. Chapman turned to me, the lone committee member not of the Interior Department, for advice. I did not yet know who the factions were in these places, but I would soon find out.

Such a mission fitted my plans nicely. I had been wanting to travel west to look at the papers of Lord Loudoun, Earl of Campbell, who had succeeded Gen. Edward Braddock as commander of the British forces in North America during the French and Indian War, at the Henry E. Huntington Library in San Marino, California. Moreover, factionalism was an emerging interest in anthropology, and here was a perfect example for intensive and comparative study. I agreed to take on the assignment. Beatty and McNickle had other ideas: McNickle wanted me to examine the progress of the Indian Reorganization Act (ira) in these settings, and Beatty suggested an aspect of Indian education. We were not of one mind.

Back at si, I called Philleo Nash, minority advisor to President Truman, who had done extensive fieldwork at Klamath and published on it. He responded with a memorandum on factionalism that briefed me on what to expect. For background on Browning,

Montana, I turned to Jack Ewers, curator of ethnology at USNM and a longtime friend from Dartmouth and Wissler's seminar at Yale, then the reigning Blackfeet specialist. Ewers, aware of the difficulties of working in Browning, was not too encouraging.

At home in Turkey Run, plans went forward for what became "the Great Western Trip." We resolved to drive to San Marino and the Huntington, come what may. We traded for a new station wagon to accommodate the whole family, including Bonner (Olive's mother), and our gear, and we rented our house while we were away.

The dimensions of our travel and my role for Interior Department lacked definition. I went into town for a final meeting of the committee. We were yet trying to accommodate the current problems of the BIA representatives to Oscar Chapman's proposal, which I now saw as a perfect design for a study of factionalism. We were still at odds when I was called to the phone. It was Olive: our son Doug, age five, had broken his arm. He had climbed a dogwood tree overlooking the driveway and descended to greet his mother too quickly coming up the drive. It was obvious where my duty lay. As I turned to go, Oscar Chapman, having heard enough discussion, came to a quick decision: he approved my project and left it to BIA to pay my travel and subsistence expenses from June 1 to Labor Day. In a compromise worked out with Darcy McNickle, I would be studying "tribal organization," which for BIA personnel meant the (IRA); and for a refresher on Indian education, I accepted Beatty's suggestion that I spend the month of June at the Santa Fe Indian School while devising a strategy for Taos Pueblo. That gave us a target for the first leg of our journey. Meanwhile, SI detailed me to BIA for three months.

We packed the new station wagon with our essential gear—kit bags for overnights in motels and a trunk on the tailgate with changes of clothes. Olive and I shared the driving while Bonner and the three children filled the two back seats. I always knew it was the end of the day and time to get off the road when the children grew restive. Doug, in a cast, rested his arm on the second seat back, and inevitably someone leaned against it and he would scream. Betsey and John developed a routine for scouting out motels: holding their noses to signal where not to stop. We followed old Route 66 from mid-continent to Santa Fe, where we found housekeeping lodgings near the Indian School.

Bonner ran the kitchen while Olive kept house. Betsey and John soon made friends with some neighboring children from Laramie, Wyoming, who taught them to play poker, the Western game. Roland Sundown, a Tonawanda Seneca who worked for the BIA and whom I had known at Dartmouth where he dressed in feathers at home games to reinforce the "Indian symbol" then in fashion and who soloed in the glee club, soon became a guest at our table. He amazed me at knowing traditional Seneca songs that he had learned as a boy in the Tonawanda Longhouse, which we recorded to our mutual satisfaction. After a stint in the Indian Service, Roland enjoyed performing for someone familiar with the Tonawanda repertoire.

Anthropologists familiar with Pueblo ethnology who dropped in at the Indian School welcomed me to the Southwest; they encouraged me to pursue my study but cautioned that I might fail to gain access to Taos.

On detail to BIA, I was expected to observe protocol. In a day or two I made an appointment with the area director and drove down to Albuquerque to meet him. I no longer recall his name, but he was well over six feet in stature and very much on the defensive, having been recently forced out of Taos. He seemed disturbed that the secretary of the interior had commissioned my study. He said he could not be responsible for my personal safety at Taos, and as a BIA person he disapproved of my proposal. I replied that my official position was at BAE–SI, that I was only on detail for expenses to BIA and that I was prepared to fail to gain access to Taos but intended to try anyway. As a professional administrator out of the University of Southern California, he had no sympathy for ethnological research, which in his view only encouraged Indians to assert their traditional ways. I had done my duty, thanked him, and left without his approval.

I settled into the routine of the BIA summer-school program at Santa Fe, where McNickle introduced me to various staff members, including Eliseo Concha, a native of Taos, whom I gradually came to know. Eliseo took a dim view of my prospects of gaining admission to the pueblo, saying that Seferino Martinez, the conservative boss, would simply order the warrior on duty to usher me out. There the matter rested for a few days, until Eliseo invited my family to visit the pueblo as guests of his family on a Sunday. We drove the sixty miles north to Taos, where Eliseo met us and ushered us from the plaza to his parents' apartment on the north side. His father, a councilor, received us in his quiet way, while Eliseo's mother stayed in the background, although interested in Olive and the children. I did not mention my proposed study, and I never knew what Eliseo had told his father.

Seferino Martinez obviously held the key to admit me to the pueblo. When I thanked Eliseo a few days later for introducing us to his parents, I proposed, "Why don't I go see Seferino myself?" Eliseo brightened and replied, "And take your family. Then you will know."

The following Sunday the warrior on duty confronted us on the Taos Pueblo plaza. I told him that the secretary of the interior had sent me to talk to Seferino Martinez. He promptly ushered us to Seferino's quarters on the south side of the plaza, where Seferino, stripped to the waist and covered with blood, was jerking beef that hung on a rack to dry, swarming with flies. Behind him a fenced enclosure held a young stallion. As I announced that Oscar Chapman had sent me to discuss the differences between the Old Men and the Boys in the pueblo (as the two factions were known), Seferino washed his hands and stood to greet me: "Oscar Chapman never sent anyone to talk with me before. BIA people come and I have them put out of the pueblo."

As we talked, I noticed the horse moving closer to the fence where son John, age eleven, was standing. Seferino saw John reach and put his hand gently on the stallion's flank and remarked, "That boy is all right; that horse would kill anyone else." John had made our day.

Speaking his native tongue, Seferino ordered two subordinates to assemble the elders to council and directed his womenfolk to make my family comfortable. In the open shed where he seated me, someone had been culling a variety of white beans. While waiting, I counted fifty beans from one pile and laid them out in the mnemonic diagram of the roll call of the sachems comprising the League of the Iroquois (Fenton 1950). I thought it might amuse the old men when they arrived and might tell them that I understood another tribal system back east.

The old men were intrigued. As I explained the league diagram, one of them remarked that the Indians in the east were all gone. Another took beans from a pile and laid out the Taos kiva diagram and tried to make me understand how it worked, a subject central to my study. I explained my mission and charge from Secretary Chapman to hear their version of the dispute between them and the Boys, and it was agreed that Seferino would serve as my tutor.

On Monday I began several days of meetings with Seferino Martinez to hear his version of the dispute between the elders and the young men who had gone off to war without heeling for jobs in the hierarchy, which was clearly a theocracy with the old men at the top. We got on nicely, and Seferino proved an excellent tutor. He was clearly "boss" of the pueblo, not unlike a character out of Lincoln Steffens.

The time of our departure from Santa Fe was fast approaching, and the leader of the other faction approached me for a hearing. We agreed to meet next day, miles away from Taos, out of hearing. The leader of the faction representing the disenfranchised "Boys" proved to be the most voluble informant I ever listened to. I made no notes as he talked—nor had I with Seferino—but dictated as much as I could recall into a tape recorder immediately on returning to Santa Fe. (One can train oneself to remember whole conversations while interviews are still fresh and nothing else intervenes.)

The next day I met Seferino crossing the plaza before reaching his digs. He greeted me by saying, "I have this ceremony on my head today," as he gestured. "I understand that you are leaving." I knew then that I had worn out my welcome at Taos. Somehow he had heard that I had listened to the opposite faction. The next autumn, on returning to Washington, I would describe how a refugee from Taos then resident in Washington helped me to write the monograph "Factionalism at Taos Pueblo" (Fenton 1957).

At the close of the session at the Santa Fe Indian School, parents from neighboring pueblos having children in the program brought drums and native foods and performed in a grand finale. It was a wonderful opportunity to hear a variety of Pueblo music, which daughter Betsey helped me record. The quality of these tapes, unfortunately, suffered from one of us having to hold the "record" lever in place.

We said good-bye to friends and colleagues, packed the car, and set out for San Marino, where Reader Services at the Huntington Library had arranged for us to rent the house of a vacationing librarian for the month of July. We made ourselves at home and enjoyed the premises. I reported at the library on July 3, the first of ten sessions up to 2002. That first summer I canvassed the papers of Lord Loudoun and of James Abercromby, his successor, to which I would return with increasing sophistication in later years as new problems arose.

In a stroke of luck for Iroquois studies and my personal library, a father and son then in charge of rare books spread out for sale odd pamphlets and unbound pages culled from the collection. I spotted unbound pages of Asher Wright's spelling book in the Seneca language, possibly the first book published in Buffalo, which I purchased for a ridiculous price.

My stint at the Huntington ended August 1, and we headed north for Klamath Reservation on the Oregon border, to resume my mission for Oscar Chapman. Klamath had a massive forest, and the feud that was taking place over its management foretold the strife of our day between environmentalists and the timber industry. After several days of briefing by the superintendent of Klamath Indian Reservation, which was most thorough and helpful, I was ready for an unofficial view.

Someone, perhaps Philleo Nash, suggested that I seek out a physician in nearby Chiloquin, a typical cow town just east of the reservation. Chiloquin boasted a movie theater, such as it was, and other amenities. I found the doctor's shingle and climbed a rickety stairway to the second floor, found his door, and sat in a well-worn chair in the waiting room. A gruff individual emerged from an equally dingy office, introduced himself, ushered me into his office, and shoved another well-worn chair in my direction. After listening to my mission, he pronounced: "The first thing you need to know about this town and reservation is that they are the greatest collection of plain and fancy sons-of-bitches in the world. I know, because I delivered them all!"

I came away thinking that interviews would be difficult. On the contrary, I found an informant of the conservative faction who proved quite reasonable. He filled me in on current activities, including the hand game, for which he had a passion. The leader of the faction that wanted to sell off the timber and run proved most difficult. I listened to her spiel for modernism without comment.

I failed to write up notes on Klamath—much to the disappointment of the superintendent—save in a comparative paper on factionalism that I later delivered in Vienna and published in the *Proceedings* of the International Congress of Anthropological and Ethnological Sciences (Fenton 1955).

While I was interviewing Indians, the family enjoyed the house and its surroundings in the natural beauty of forest and river. Betsey and John joined agency kids in trying to catch escaped fish from the upstream hatchery, while Doug, in cowboy boots and hat, now out of his cast, tagged along. We were soon joined by Joe Weckler of UCLA, whom we had known from the war years at the Smithsonian, an avid fly fisherman who came up to Klamath to try the neighboring waters. Joe brought a sleeping bag and slept on the floor several nights. He came back one night with some beautiful trout that had taken his flies in Crater Lake and stashed them in the refrigerator until he returned to Los Angeles.

We had all turned in for the night when Joe let out a howl: "Those damned children!" John and Betsey, tired of his criticism of their behavior and his complaints to their parents that we had no control of them, had slipped several cold trout into his sleeping bag. Next day, in a show of parental control, I sentenced the two to yard work—mowing and raking the grounds.

As a family we visited some of the local sights, including Crater Lake, where Joe Weckler had caught the trout, in the bottom of a now extinct volcano within its own national park. The view from the rim is spectacular. I was not then a fly fisherman, so I was not tempted to look for the path down.

It was now mid-August and time to head north toward the Blackfeet Reservation in Montana. I had learned all I could about factionalism at Klamath in the time available.

Having visited the redwoods of northern California on the way to Klamath and passed the month of August in the Klamath forest, we headed north through Oregon, ferried over the Columbia River in Washington, and crossed the Continental Divide near Glacier National Park to descend into Browning, Montana, and the Blackfeet Agency. It was already September and our visit would be short.

The agent installed us in a schoolteacher's residence, where the schoolyard afforded swings and slides, which the first evening Blackfeet children rode in to use, leaving their mounts to forage unattended. John and Betsey were soon mounted on Blackfeet ponies while Indian children enjoyed the swings and slides. John never would recover from his love of horses.

The main street of Browning leading to the post office was lined with old men sitting in front of stores, waiting for passing relatives to give them a handout. Leadership in Blackfeet society depended on generosity. The theme ran: "You are a Chief, give!" Begging had gotten to be a fine art. Not surprisingly, expectation of generosity permeated Blackfeet politics. The faction in power maintained itself by the Plains Indian ethic of giving, not unlike some political machines of urban America. What to the outsider appeared a corrupt, Tammany-like system of buying votes and maintaining leadership by awarding plums to constituents developed as a natural consequence of social relations. I interviewed a rising leader of the progressive faction, who explained the difficulties of operating within the Indian Reorganization Act constitution, given the expectations of his people.

Postmaster Taliafero, an old Virginia name, told me how Julia Wades-in-water reduced begging to a fine art. Summers she kept an autograph book of names and addresses of visitors to Browning and Glacier Park. Winters, she mined the book for charity, writing letters telling how cold it was, how people were starving and dying. Gifts of clothes and money orders poured into the Browning post office. "Another Julia Wades-in-water" became a watchword for any large parcel-post package I shoved through the post office window. Anticipating the long trip home, we mailed our spare clothing.

Within a week of our arrival, Felix Cohen, attorney for the BIA, whom we knew socially as parents of schoolchildren in Washington and with whom I had discussed protocol in Indian claims, arrived in Browning to present amendments to the IRA constitution, which he had drafted and the Blackfeet had accepted.[4] Felix introduced us to Ross Hagerty, a prominent rancher married to a Blackfeet woman, himself of Indian heritage by his mother. Of a Sunday, Felix guided us north to the Hagerty ranch, spread out along the boundary with Canada. As we approached, I noticed a herd of some fifty Palomino horses grazing on the range. When I later remarked to Ross on his herd, he told me of an old Indian who owned over a hundred horses, and when asked by the agent why he had so many, the old man replied, "I just love horses."

Felix as usual was all business. While he and Ross discussed revisions in the IRA constitution, I listened. Olive and Ross's wife found things to talk about, and Betsey and John disappeared into the working quarters of the ranch, where ranch hands found them bridles and saddles and mounted them on fine steeds within the corral. They were doing nicely when Ross, Olive, and I found them. As Betsey rode by, Ross remarked, "She is doing fine. That horse threw me yesterday." His comment was not very reassuring to her parents.

We stayed for dinner. The children ate steaks with the ranch hands in the bunkhouse while we dined inside. Ross entertained us with tales of his travels by rail to Washington before air flights. To pass the days he packed a satchel with silver dollars for the poker game, which ended in Washington and resumed on the return trip.

At some point I asked Ross to meet with me in Browning during the week when he came to town. His reply underscored what I had already learned: "I can't afford to go to Browning. My relatives are lined up expecting me to give them money."

As we departed, Ross advised us to head east for home, since any day we might expect a September snowstorm if the wind shifted, and then not a wheel would turn for days.

In our short stay in Browning I had barely scratched the surface. But on returning to Washington in late September, at the request of the Indian Bureau, I drafted a plan for the study of the Blackfeet problem by a team of social scientists drawn from several disciplines including anthropology. It never came off.

Having made every effort to lighten the load, we packed our gear, with fossil-bearing rocks that John and Betsey insisted on taking home under the seats, left Cut Bank Creek behind us, and headed east toward Great Falls. We were thrilled to see bison grazing on the range and close by the roadside in the Big Sky country of eastern Montana. Somewhere in the Badlands the car began to sway. The rear tires were giving out from the load, and the right rear tire was nearly flat. No cars were in sight, but Betsey and John posted themselves front and rear with towels to flag any passing cars while I jacked up the car and changed tires. When later I complained to the Washington Ford dealer, he remarked that I was using the car as a two-ton truck.

Swan Song at BAE

Ensconced once again at the Smithsonian in the fall of 1950, I found professional activities beginning to assume a larger role in my life. I joined the executive board of the American Anthropological

Association during the presidency of Morris Edward Opler, whose articles on the theory of themes I had published as editor of the *Journal of the Washington Academy of Sciences,* and I continued to serve under Leslie White. That exposure led to other things.

The Fentons enjoyed the summer of 1951 at Ann Arbor, where I was visiting professor of anthropology at the University of Michigan. My lecture section in general anthropology met in the basement of Angel Hall, which was being renovated, and the constant din of jackhammers made it impossible for students to hear. My assistant, Beth Wilder, daughter of a distinguished mathematician and a disciple of Leslie White, suggested that I run movies and invite the construction workers to sit in. They agreed to suspend the racket for twenty minutes each morning until I could get my point across. I taught typical Boasian anthropology, including Benedict's patterns of culture and Sapir's personality and culture. Leslie White, to his credit, never objected, although these topics were anathema to him.

The first day of the course, the back row was filled with handsome young men who resembled Ivy Leaguers of my day. After I announced a term paper in lieu of a final exam, they all vanished. They were summer football players, I was told, looking for a pipe course.

Hans and Gertrude Kurath made certain that we were at home in Ann Arbor. They introduced us to Crystal Lake, where anthropologists and linguists gathered Sundays to picnic and swim. John and Betsey teamed up with the Kurath children, Eddie and Ellen, who labeled Doug the DP, or "Dougie problem." One Sunday the children staged a satire on the scholars by swimming to a convenient depth and gesturing with their hands to the point of submerging. Another time Gertrude arrived by swimming the lake to proclaim, "Hans is coming with the beer."

Gertrude and I were collaborating on the Iroquois Eagle Dance, she doing the choreography and I the ethnohistory. Library resources at the university afforded abundant comparative material on the related Calumet Dance, which I exploited as the summer term wound down.

I extended our stay in Ann Arbor to examine manuscripts relating to the political history of the Iroquois Confederacy, notably the Gage Papers at the William L. Clements Library. There I met Helen Hornbeck Tanner, who later became my colleague and friend at the Newberry Library. Helen had read all of the Gage Papers and helped me to find items crucial to my interest.

In October, back in Washington, I organized and conducted the Seventh Conference on Iroquois Research, which met at Red House, New York. I recall two significant presentations of this period: Anthony F. C. Wallace's "The Dekanawidah Epic Analyzed as a Revitalization Movement" and Annemarie Shimony's "Conservatism at Six Nations."

By then I was known for having used ethnological findings for interpreting historical sources, and the organizers of a symposium on the training of professional anthropologists invited me to present my views on the training of historical anthropologists at the annual meeting of the American Anthropological Association in Chicago. Margaret Mead, arriving as I was speaking, picked up where I left off, saying, "Bill Fenton says we should all learn to use card catalogs." I hope I said more than that.

I wound up my thirteen years of research at the Bureau of American Ethnology by delivering the Eagle Dance monograph to the editors for publication and resigned my position as of December 31, 1951. My future rested with the National Research Council. How I got there had much to do with the nation's Cold War fears of the bomb.

9. Bill Fenton and his Voightlander camera.

10. Wolf Run on the Allegheny River, 1933.

11. Photograph by Bill Fenton of some of his Seneca "family," from the Hawk Clan, and their spouses, 1933.

12. Chauncey Johnny John preparing a hoop for a game, 1933.

13. Sherman Redeye (*left*), who "got it right," and Bill, 1934.

14. Bill's faithful Packard, 1936.

15. Jemima Gibson finds
pneumonia medicine, 1939.

16. The Hilton Hills and Olive
Fenton (*center*) at Her Majesty's
Chapel to the Mohawks,
Brantford, Ontario, 1939.

17. Beaver Clan women, Nephew lineage, 1947 .

18. Beaver Clan spouses and Fenton adoptees, 1947.

FIVE

The National Research Council

Late in November 1951, the Division of Anthropology and Psychology of the National Research Council asked me to help organize a conference on disaster studies, a concern of the research branch of the Department of Defense dealing with how the American public might react to an atomic attack. The Department of Defense was prepared to fund future studies, and NRC would impanel a committee and oversee the research. The Division of Anthro and Psych, having decided to appoint an executive secretary—a full-time job with a salary greater than that of a research position at the Smithsonian—had interviewed several candidates, and in the course of our preparations for the conference, I became one. S. S. "Smitty" Stevens, then chairman of the division—a hard-nosed experimental psychologist and professor at Harvard—came down from Cambridge to interview me. Smitty took a dim view of anthropology as science but decided I was a communicator, and the fact that I had once been a skier at Dartmouth convinced him that I might do a creditable job. We kept in touch by telephone.

The conference was set for December 6. Responsibility lay with Anthro and Psych (what people might do in a disaster was clearly a problem for the behavioral sciences), but the observers of the aftermath of the atomic strikes in Japan had been physicians, and so the Division of Medicine also felt a responsibility for the questions the conference would address. The Division of Medicine enjoyed a long-standing relationship with the research branch of the Department of Defense. It was headed by Dean Winternitz, late of Yale Medical School and a terror to his students, who called on me to size me up and urge the sharing of responsibility for the upcoming conference because, in his view, the real experts were physicians. After some discussion we reached a guarded understanding. Later we became friends.

Real trouble lay ahead. I failed to persuade Smitty, who was in the midst of some experiment, to come down from Cambridge and chair the conference. He delegated responsibility to Loren Eiseley, vice-chairman of the division, whom I knew as a graceful writer and colleague and whom I trusted had the necessary skills to chair a meeting. I was mistaken.

Eiseley was inclined to listen rather than comment, and he soon lost control of the conference, while I sat behind him powerless to define the issues for my superior. Dean Winternitz took over. Defense Department representatives wondered, would the American public panic in an atomic disaster? Physicians, mainly concerned with radiation burns, said little about human behavior in the aftermath of Hiroshima and Nagasaki. Someone suggested the British experience during the London Blitz as a model. (I made a note of that.) Obviously, no real experts on behavior in extreme situations were present that day. We would have to find or train them.

The first conference on disaster studies had not gone well, and the front office of the National Academy and the NRC was embarrassed: both my division and I were in trouble.

Smitty must have defended me, however, because I was appointed executive secretary of the Division of Anthropology and Psychology as of January 1, 1952, and the Committee on Disaster Studies was assigned to my division under a new chairman, the psychologist Carlyle "Jake" Jacobson, dean of medicine at the State University of New York (SUNY) Upstate Medical Center, a man of strong background in primatology and administration. Smitty, Jake, and I put together a team of behavioral scientists who set about defining the problem and deciding what could be researched. The group opted for behavior in natural disasters such as tornadoes and floods and possibly an assessment of the British experience during the Blitz of London.

Word went out to the community of behavioral scientists. Anthony Wallace, one of the more innovative minds in anthropology, came down from Philadelphia to find out what I was doing in my new position, particularly disaster studies. He listened as I outlined the state of the art: we were seeking analogs of human behavior in extreme situations; because there were no experts in the field, we would have to find them or train them; and we were looking for people who had observed human behavior in the aftermath of tornadoes and floods. Tony returned to Philadelphia and worked on a model for the study of human behavior in such situations, which he later modified in his study of the 1956 Worcester, Massachusetts, tornado.[1]

On firmer ground, I was now responsible for Mel Herskovits's Committee on International Relations in Anthropology, which he had created in 1946. Herskovits, having worked in Africa before the war, had urged American anthropologists to widen their horizons beyond North and Middle America. Foreseeing greater public interest in the rest of the world and with a concern to assist colleagues in war-torn countries, he recruited Henry Collins and me from the Ethnogeographic Board and Professors Robert Heine-Geldern, who had come to New York when the Nazis annexed Austria, and Alfred Métraux, my colleague at the Smithsonian and a refugee from Nazism in France, to help form the new committee at the NRC. Professor Frederica de Laguna (Bryn Mawr) joined us presently. The committee had two principal concerns: the plight of our colleagues abroad, to which Heine-Geldern and Métraux had alerted us, and American participation in the International Congress of Anthropological and Ethnological Sciences (ICAES).[2]

The committee had now reached a mature stage and was reaching out to colleagues overseas who, during the war years, had been stripped of freedom to pursue independent research and cut off from advances elsewhere. The committee decided to inventory the state of anthropology in affected countries, hoping to give some encouragement to colleagues who had missed out on recent developments in the discipline. Each member accepted an area or country to inventory; I took the Arab world of the Near East because I knew that Afif Tannous, my former student at St. Lawrence University, then at the State Department, had the necessary contacts and would help. Tannous, a native of Lebanon and alumnus of the American University at Beirut, took me to the Washington residence of Costi Zurack, a Lebanese diplomat, on the eve of his departure for home. Zurack, a sometime academic, ticked off names of academics in Lebanon and neighboring countries while answering the pleas of letter writers in every corner of the room to deliver their letters. I sensed the strong bonds of kinship in the Arab world.

Tannous and I interviewed other Near Eastern scholars as they visited Washington or departed for home, charged with queries on our behalf. Sketchy as it may have been, my report to the committee, "Anthropology during the War, VII: The Arab World," appeared in the *American Anthropologist* (Fenton 1947).

London and Cambridge, 1952

American participation in the International Congress of Anthropological and Ethnological Sciences centered in the Committee on International Relations in Anthropology, and the congress would hold its first meeting since the war in Vienna in 1952. Robert Heine-Geldern would be the host, and Mel Herskovits was scheduled to lead the American delegation as the U.S. delegate, appointed by the secretary of state. But a Mrs. Shipman, in charge of such matters at the State Department, had other ideas. Mel phoned me in obvious distress to say that Mrs. Shipman objected to his liberal politics and had turned down the NRC's recommendation; would I take his place? Mel knew that I had the necessary clearance. He would fight the denial of his appointment, but time would expire before he succeeded in wiping the dishonor from his slate. I agreed to go in his place.

The NRC forwarded my name to the State Department, Mrs. Shipman evidently liked what she saw, and I was duly appointed U.S. delegate to the ICAES, replete with certificate and special passport signed on behalf of the secretary of state. I requested early passage to London in July in order to learn what I could about the British experience during the Blitz and attend the International Congress of Americanists in Cambridge in early August before going on to Vienna for the ICAES in September. This would be my first travel abroad, and preparations required quick decisions.

My friend Paul Oehser reminded me that the Saville Club of London offered an "exchange of amenities" with the Cosmos Club, of which he was secretary. Paul wrote requesting accommodations for me during July, which were granted. The NRC got me accredited to the Science Office at the U.S. embassy on Grosvenor Square, so I had a base of operations, near the club on Brook Street. By a stroke of luck, a London psychiatrist visiting NRC stopped by my office to hear about disaster studies and offered assistance in meeting key personnel in London.

It was now late in June, and Washington was sweltering in muggy weather. I bid good-bye to my family and went to the airport, where a State Department official handed me tickets and special passport as I mounted the ladder of a TWA Constellation—a four-engine monoplane—for my first trans-Atlantic flight. I was wearing a cotton seersucker suit and straw hat, uniform of the day in the nation's capital.

The temperature was some 50 degrees F. and breezy when I stepped out at Heathrow in my summer suit, but the Saville Club porter, on whom I came to depend, installed me in a front room furnished in Regency furniture and drew me a hot tub in my private bathroom—a unique luxury I would soon learn. I awoke to the clop-clop of the horse guard on the way from stables to parade at Buckingham Palace, a morning call on Brook Street. The club porter greeted me with tea and biscuits and hung up my suits in the mahogany wardrobe, remarking that one of the members might introduce me to his tailor, who could make me a proper suit during my stay.

At breakfast I met Roger Tory Peterson, the ornithologist, originally of Jamestown, New York, who immediately linked me with Reuben E. Fenton, Civil War governor of New York, a remote relative of my grandfather William T., farmer of Conewango Valley, but dating back to England, where, I would soon learn, all the Fentons had originated. Peterson was in London working on a book on birds of Britain with Dermot Wilson, his sponsor at the Saville.

Eggs for breakfast were still in scarce supply in London, but affiliation with the Science Office at the U.S. embassy afforded access to the PX, where eggs were plentiful. I took a dozen back to the Saville and gave them to the steward. Next morning he asked, "Sir, would you like one of your eggs?" I had intended to share them with other residents.

The visiting London psychiatrist had given me his telephone number and told me to call him when settled in London. The club steward rang him for me, and he immediately invited me to dine at home with him and his wife. It was a memorable evening, my first as a guest in an English home. He inquired about my background, and I recited the family legend of John Carr, father of great-grandmother Fanny Carr and seventh son of the Earl of Cessford, Scotland. He immediately turned to Burke's Peerage, but no such earl was listed. So much for family folklore.

We next turned to a mutual interest in disaster studies and planning a strategy for my inquiries about the British experience during the Blitz. He advised me to start with the home minister, Sir Ernest Rock-Carling, whom he immediately rang up at home. Suddenly I had an appointment with a man I had never even hoped to meet.

The club steward, who had an uncanny sense for sizing up situations, having learned my appointment was for eleven o'clock, predicted just what would happen when I arrived in an embassy car. There would be two officers posted at the curb to receive me and usher me into the Home Office. However, uncertain that my status with the Science Office warranted an embassy car, I demurred and requested a London cab. The steward was right. When the cab pulled up at the curb of the Home Office, two puzzled officers asked why I was there. When I identified myself, one remarked, "We were expecting an embassy car."

The Home Office, rather modest by Washington standards, occupied the second floor of a gray stone building of uncertain age. The home officer's secretary led me into a room furnished in the eighteenth-century mode with period furniture. While Sir Ernest was on the telephone, I admired a grandfather clock to the left of his desk from where I sat. Sensing my interest, the minister put down the phone and remarked, "That clock was ticking in this office when Marie Antoinette was beheaded across the channel."

The home minister proceeded to open doors for me to visit key officials who during the Blitz had pooled jurisdictions for the duration in the interest of assisting the London public to endure an extreme situation. Within twenty-four hours I would receive detailed instructions with bus numbers and departure times to reach the London County Council across the Thames and interview its chief executive. Londoners, whether cab drivers, civil servants, or ministers, know their city and excel at logistics; it always amazes me how they cope with its many jurisdictions, which so bewilder a foreigner.

At the London County Council next day I learned how the several jurisdictions that make up London had relinquished control of their independent fire companies and police officers, though only on the consideration that independence be restored after the war. This was the first indication I had of the way people focus in an extreme situation. I was to hear repeatedly: "We were never better off emotionally than during the Blitz."

I settled into a routine of mornings on disaster studies, afternoons at the British Museum and Library, and evenings at the Saville Club. At the library I canvassed the Haldimand Papers, to which I would return in later years, and I came to know several of the "regulars" at Saville. A senior resident and longtime editor of *The Lancet* approached me one evening to say, "Just because we don't make a fuss over you, don't think that you are not welcome." Later he remarked, "Perhaps you may be related to Sir Geoffrey Fenton, a member of Saville. I'll introduce you next time he comes in." Several nights later Sir Geoffrey appeared, and we were introduced. He asked about my roots in England and said, "Perhaps we are related; all the Fentons come from up on 'the Wash'"—the northeast coast of England. I learned afterward that Sir Geoffrey was surgeon to the queen.

Snooker, rather than billiards, the Cosmos passion, had its addicts at the Saville Club, and I came to know some of the players, although the fine points of the game escaped me. One player drove an antique car that had to be hand cranked and choked manually until the engine let out a great roar that filled Brook Street, just as the club steward locked the front door at 10:15 and I was turning in for the night.

Colleagues in London soon learned that I was replacing Mel Herskovits as the U.S. delegate to the ICAES in Vienna. Professor Daryl Forde, who knew Herskovits, had expected him and was familiar with American politics from a year in the United States, demanded to know why I, a relatively unknown person, was there instead. Without going into details, I told Forde that Mel, unable to attend, had asked me to take his place, which was the truth, though Forde appeared to remain unconvinced.

It was the last week of July, and the Thirtieth International Congress of Americanists was soon to open in Cambridge. With so many anthropologists in town, the venerable Royal Anthropological Institute hosted a sherry party in Bedford Square. Having been

introduced around, in the midst of the crowd I found myself standing next to a tweedy gentleman, somewhat the worse for wear, to
whom I acknowledged that it was gracious of the Duke of Bedford
to let the institute hold its party in the square. Adrian Digby, then
assistant keeper of ethnography at the British Museum, who came
by to rescue me, said, "That was His Grace you were talking to."

Participants at the Americanist Congress were expected to deliver
papers. During my final week at the Saville, before the club closed
for the month of August, I wrote a fifteen-minute paper on stability of cultural patterns among American Indians, later published
in *Journal of the Royal Anthropological Institute* (Fenton 1953). The
club steward installed me in a third-floor room where there was a
writing desk with good light. Pausing between sentences, I looked
down at a nameplate that read: "The writing desk of H. G. Wells."
I hoped my prose might measure up.

When the club closed, Adrian Digby took me home to Saffron
Walden, an ancient village in East Anglia where a street of store-
fronts displayed representations of ancient trades above their doors.
Adrian, Nicky, and two daughters made me at home and hosted a
sherry party for guests en route to Cambridge, including several
who would also be in Vienna. As the time approached, the Digbys
and their houseguests all converged on Cambridge.

Geoffrey Bushnell—Cambridge don, prehistorian, and noted
wit—met us, parked his 1910 vintage black bicycle in a doorway,
and after leading us on a brief tour of Roman ruins, on which
he was the acknowledged authority, escorted us to Johns College
at the top of High Street, where most of the Americanists were
lodged. The registrar of the college came in presently to assign
us quarters. Attendants from the Continent, ahead of me in the
queue, invariably opted for rooms in the new north wing of the
court. When my turn came, the registrar remarked, "I presume
the Yankee will choose modern quarters?" I replied, "No, as a
first-time visitor to Cambridge, I would like to experience living
in the old college."

He assigned me to rooms on the "back," overlooking the River
Cam and passing punters. Few of the wrought-iron casement windows really closed, having been forced and bent out of shape. To
the east one looked out on the court, or keep, that one crossed to
the baths, an adventure in winter requiring agility and a woolen
English bathrobe. Below I beheld from an east window a scene out

of the Middle Ages: a stonemason repairing the cobblestone walkway, leveling in fresh sand the cobbles that his young apprentice selected from a small wooden wheelbarrow. With a short-handled hammer, he tapped each stone into place. At night, one could hear the college bells strike the hour the length of High Street to Trinity College on the south.

Breakfast next morning in the great hall of Johns College proved a daunting but inspiring experience. I took my place at a long wooden table facing a window. As I looked up from my porridge and read the names of the Johns College worthies, a panel devoted to John Eliot caught my eye. Eliot, who attended Cambridge in the 1630s and became a missionary to the Massachusett Algonquians, translated the New Testament into the Massachusett language in 1663. The memorial made me realize how relatively recent are the colleges of the Ivy League—Yale 1701, Princeton 1746, Dartmouth 1769.

The congress convened briefly the first afternoon, so that our host might welcome us, and adjourned in less than an hour to the nearest pub. The second afternoon, I read the paper I had written, and the next morning at breakfast, two puzzled Germans who had survived the Nazi regime approached me and asked to read a copy of it. I asked, "Could you not understand me?" One of them replied, "Not entirely. You sounded like your late president, but you did not articulate as clearly." To this partial compliment I explained that I had never realized the resemblance, although President Roosevelt and I both came from the same part of New York State.

Johns College hosted a grand dinner in its great hall and set the tables with the silver service attributed to a bequest from the mother of Henry VIII. Great silver basins of water with floating rose petals graced the center of two rows of long tables, within arm's reach of guests, for washing their hands. Alfred Kidder II—son of A. V. Kidder and better known as Ted—with his wife, Mary, sat with me near the Eliot window, where the college butler between courses counted the great soup spoons from our table, washed them in a silver bowl atop a sideboard, restored them to their felt bags, and loaded a trolley, which a servant wheeled back into the vault. Adrian Digby demonstrated for us how early guests washed food from their faces and hands.

The Master of Johns, Francis Bartlett, eminent psychologist of "memory" fame, presided at the high table. Bartlett had visited the Smithsonian in 1948 while attending a bicentennial celebration at Princeton, and Secretary Wetmore, not knowing what to do with him, detailed me to usher him around and deliver him to the Cosmos Club at lunchtime. Bartlett remembered me and agreed to meet next afternoon to hear about the NRC's concern with human behavior during disasters. We met next day in the master's quarters. When I related that I had been inquiring about the "British experience" during the Blitz, Bartlett commented, "We were never better off emotionally; there was virtually no neurosis, far less than at present. The threat was clear, and people were focused." That summed it up as far as I was concerned.

The college porter manages the goings and comings of the residents and fulfills their needs so long as in his judgment they conform to the rules. There being no telephone in my rooms, I appealed to this austere figure for assistance in telephoning my wife in Virginia before going on to Vienna. It is difficult to appreciate today what a transatlantic phone call involved fifty years ago. The national government monopolized such calls; one had to reserve a time; and conversations were staggered—one spoke, stating the business, and then the recipient might reply. It was no game for husband and wife used to immediate answers. Consequently, beyond hearing Olive's voice, I learned little.

The college porter told me to go back to my rooms and he would come and get me when a line opened. I waited a half hour. Presently I sighted the porter in top hat and formal jacket crossing the court, and then I heard him mounting the stairs to my quarters. He knocked, doffed his hat and announced, "Your call, Sir, is ready." We returned to the lodge and I picked up the phone to hear a male operator instruct me how to proceed.

Geoffrey Turner, of the Pitt-Rivers Museum at Oxford, had sent me his studies describing objects in the museum's collection from northeastern America, their technology, and art. Geoffrey sought me out at the congress and introduced me to Beatrice Blackwood, curator of the Pitt-Rivers, who invited me to share the drive to Oxford—some eighty miles—which I readily accepted.

Next morning, I was packed and ready to go at nine o'clock outside the main gateway to Johns College. On the way out I paused at the porter's lodge to thank him for his kindness during my stay, when he remarked to an assistant, "That's the chap who phoned his old woman in the States," which he pronounced "Stites." He then asked me, "What ever happened to Professor Bateson's (Biteson's) son? He went off to the South Seas and sent back stuff that fills a room at the back of the college. We never heard of or saw him again. I suppose the natives must have et him." I assured him that Gregory Bateson was much alive and in the States when last I saw him.

"Beatie" Blackwood and Geoffrey Turner came by Johns College gate at the appointed hour to pick me up for the drive to Oxford. Beatie's open Austin, which had served her while she was air-raid warden of Oxford during the Blitz, was already crammed full of their luggage, not to mention the Oxford Aztec Codex, which had been on view during the congress, but she managed to make room for me and my gear. It was dark when we reached Oxford, but Beatie rang up the keeper of manuscripts at the Bodleian Library at home to come in and open the vault so she could return the codex. Such casual handling of a cultural treasure amazed me; in the United States its transport would have required an armored car and police escort.

Next morning I met the head keeper of the Pitt-Rivers Museum at tea, after which Beatie and Geoffrey gave me a quick tour of the collections. I particularly remember seeing for the first time the wampum that Horatio Hale had sent to E. B. Tylor, then the recently appointed keeper of the University Museum, famed for his definition of "culture."

At noon we three were invited to lunch at the home of Sir Francis and Lady Knowles. Francis H. S. Knowles, Bart., had come out to Canada in 1912, when Edward Sapir recruited him for the Anthropological Survey of Canada and assigned him to the Iroquois team to study the skeletal remains that Wintemberg had excavated at the Roebuck site, a prehistoric Iroquois village in northeast Ontario. Knowles then measured the largest living Iroquoian population in Canada at Six Nations reserve on Grand River and, finding them a mixed lot, turned to the Tonawanda Band of Senecas, whom he found most nearly resembled the prehistoric Iroquois of Roebuck. Sir Francis and I had corresponded on Iroquois matters for several years (1944–52, Fenton Papers, APSL). I had most recently sent him a cheddar cheese from the Mohawk Valley, in view of the prevailing austerity in Britain just then, hoping he would share it with Oxford colleagues.

The streets running north from Oxford toward Banbury Cross are lined with yellow brick family residences built during the late Victorian era, including the Knowles residence. Beatie and Geoffrey were frequent visitors there and old friends. I no longer recall what was served for lunch, only that it was sumptuous for the times, and Sir Francis capped it off by slicing the cheese that I had sent, for which they were most grateful. We stayed a while after lunch to hear Sir Francis recall his fieldwork among the Iroquois of Canada and western New York. Leaving, I spotted a large engraving of a naval battle in the Baltic, for the heroics at which an ancestor had been knighted with the title that Sir Francis inherited.

Next day, thanks again to the intervention of Beatie Blackwood, I was admitted as a reader to the Bodleian Library. In my perennial quest for sources on the Iroquois, I looked at the Clarendon papers, which E. B. O'Callaghan had used in preparing the New York Colonial Documents (1853–87). Manuscripts at the Bodleian were bound in large folio volumes that were chained to the shelves with leashes long enough to enable a reader to take the volume to a nearby table. An aisle of such chained volumes presented a formidable sight. I made a few notes but decided to rely on the printed text. I took the train to London and arranged to fly to Vienna.

ICAES Vienna, 1952

British Airways flew me to Vienna, with one stop in Switzerland. The high-wing, two-engine monoplane afforded an excellent view of the countryside, dotted with picturesque villages, as we approached Zurich airport at low altitude. Unlike in the United States, where we mow strips between runways and abandon the clippings, thrifty Swiss peasant farmers were raking recently cut grass and loading high, two-wheel carts drawn by single horses, presumably as feed for livestock. Wooden rakes and forks were their principal implements.

A young State Department official named Robbins, who was assigned to me, met my plane and drove me to the Hotel Bristol in Vienna. Americans had taken over this one-time British establishment. Russians occupied an adjacent hotel, and the French were elsewhere, as were the British, for Vienna was then occupied by the four allied powers. I would soon learn that the Viennese turned out to cheer at the changing-of-the-guard ceremony when the Russians relinquished control to the Americans, for they had reason to remember the invasion from the east.

Once I presented my special passport, which established my credentials as the U.S. delegate to the congress, I couldn't open a door without some hotel or other doorman interceding on my behalf. I soon got used to this bit of deference.

Ted Crowfoot of Westport, Connecticut, whom I had known at Compo Beach in the 1920s and who held a post at the embassy in Vienna (no telling where the Compo Beach boys would show up), soon called to say that the cast of *Porgy and Bess* had arrived in town and that the embassy had planned to do something to honor me—would I mind sharing the event with the cast, who were also staying at the Bristol? I would receive tickets to the opening. Of course I agreed, knowing the tickets to the initial performance were at a premium.

I was introduced by an embassy official, and I told the guests, who were mostly members of the cast, why I was in Vienna. I was followed by Cab Calloway, of the cast, who proceeded to conduct an impromptu performance that involved nearly everyone present. Leontyne Price sang arias from the opera, followed by several others solo and in chorus, when Cab himself was not sharing some hit from his own repertoire, like "Minnie the Moocher." It was the party of a lifetime.

Breakfast next morning at the Bristol was equally memorable. The headwaiter seated me with Cab Calloway and Senator Connally of Texas, whose name Austrians accented on the penultimate syllable. Three people of more divergent interests cannot be imagined, but we managed a lively conversation on several topics of the day.

The opening day of the congress was unmemorable. Robert Heine-Geldern, as host and president, introduced the national delegates—Vinigi Grotanelli (Italy), E. E. Evans-Pritchard (United Kingdom), and myself, among others. There was no representative of the Soviet Union present. Alfred Métraux was the sole representative of France that I recall.

Among the Americans present were the archaeologists Marie Wormington and Ted Kidder. The Austrians included Father Schmidt, out-dated cultural theorist, and colleagues of the Holy Word, notably Martin Gusinde, of Feuerlander fame; Anna Hohenwart-Gerlachstein, erstwhile Hapsburg nobility and assistant to Heine-Geldern; and Etta Becker-Donner, aspiring curator of the Museum fur Volkerkunde. Besides Daryll Forde (London), Evans-Pritchard (Oxford) represented the United Kingdom. Herman Baldus, expatriate German, was there for Brazil, and the Norwegian Thor Heyerdahl, of uncertain status, was much in evidence. The permanent council that governs the congress met that afternoon. As the meeting dragged, Evans-Pritchard, in an aside to me, remarked that he would prefer hearing the Vienna Boys Choir rehearse at St. Stefanskirche.

Sessions began next day. I had prepared a paper titled "Factionalism in American Indian Societies," based on my recent fieldwork, which was scheduled that morning at eleven. I was amazed to see the lecture room fill up with Austrians. Alfred Métraux came up to the rostrum, greatly amused, to tell me, "They all expect to hear about Karl May"—a writer who had never visited North America but who wrote best-selling novels about American Indians that German readers imagined were real. The paper went well, nobody walked out, and it appeared later in the *Proceedings* (Fenton 1955).

I skipped hearing papers the next day to visit the cathedral, view the Breugel sketches of peasant games in the Hofburg, and call at the offices of anthropology high-up in the Spanische Reitschule nearby. From the Reitschule's upper gallery one can watch the famous stallions in rehearsal.

Paul Fejos, then director of the Wenner-Gren Foundation, was on hand with a stack of crisp twenty-dollar bills, ready to assist any member of the U.S. delegation short of funds. Fejos, an ex-officer of a Hungarian cavalry regiment during the late Hapsburg reign, gloried in the scene of his younger manhood. He recalled that era as we sat in a street-side park memorializing famous musicians of Alt Wien, notably Beethoven, Mozart, and Strauss. I never had enough of Vienna, and anthropology would take me there again, twice in later years.

The congress over, Alfred Métraux and I caught the afternoon flight to Paris, which was quite rough over the Alps, but Alfred assured me that Air France never spilled a glass of wine. I stopped over for a few days in Paris, with Alfred as my gracious guide, to visit the UNESCO offices and the Bibliotheque Nationale, where I hoped to see the famous "Paris Document of 1666" depicting the clans of the Senecas. (Fenton, "Northern Iroquoian," 1978: 299).

Fortunately, it was on view in a flat case where we could examine it. I also found time to visit the Musee de l'Homme that afternoon to see the collection of seventeenth- and eighteenth-century Huron-Iroquois clothing that had been collected for the edification of the Dauphin. Later I would bring some of it to Albany for a show at the New York State Museum.

A Summer in New England and a Career Move

After the academic year 1952–53, Olive and I decided that, my having spent the previous summer abroad while the family sweltered in Virginia, the whole family was due a summer outing together down East. We chose northern New England, where we had several invitations to visit. For nearly a decade, Ernest Dodge and Wendell Hadlock, both Maine native sons, and I had pursued research interests in native Indian watercraft—Dodge and I in elmbark and Hadlock in birchbark canoes—and both men were fun to be around. Hadlock found us a cottage on a rocky spit in Rockport Harbor where his father operated a lobster pound, and we rented it for a week. Dodge arranged for us to stay at a bird sanctuary in Topsfield, Massachusetts. Besides, Smitty Stevens, my boss at NRC, insisted we stop with him and his wife, Didi, at their summer place in New Hampshire, and Gene and Sally Magenau expected us not to bypass Ragged Mountain Club on the way home.

We left Ed Kennard and his wife in charge of Bassie, our cat, and our Turkey Run home and headed down East toward Maine. We stopped in Freeport long enough to visit L. L. Bean's store, which had expanded considerably in recent years, and settled into the cottage that Wendell had found for our stay. Although busy building a house for his family, Wendell introduced us to Rockport sights, including his father's lobster pound. Captain Hadlock selected two fine lobsters for us and instructed us how to prepare them. Several of us still remember the feast on our rocky spit, when seagulls screamed overhead and dived on scraps that we threw to them.

Accommodations at the bird sanctuary in Topsfield were minimal, but the ambiance afforded John much to explore, including a pond teeming with aquatic life. One day I returned from a day with Ernest Dodge at the Peabody Museum to discover that he had caught a sunfish of record proportions. Although we respected the sanctuary for birds, the pond was not posted.

For me the summer was not entirely for recreation. I took a day to drive to Albany to consult with Carlyle Jacobsen on some matters affecting the Committee on Disaster Studies (the offices of the State University were then in the state capitol). Jake was always pleasant, and we soon discharged our business. Time to spare, I crossed Washington Avenue to the State Education Building, took the elevator to the fifth floor to the State Museum, and called on Carl Guthe, then director. Guthe had, as chairman of the division that I served at NRC, been a founder of the Ethnogeorahic Board during the war, and he was interested to learn what brought me to Albany. After I filled him in on current activities of the division and told him about my findings in London and Cambridge the previous summer, including my role in the Vienna congress, he confided that after ten years and a heart ailment, he was about to resign his post. Meanwhile, the position of assistant director was open. Would I be interested? I said no, that I liked what I was doing. (Actually, I didn't want to be assistant director of anything.) Guthe went on to say that a national search was under way for a director. With this news in mind I drove back to Topsfield.

That evening the Dodges and Fentons supped together. I naturally related what I had discovered in Albany. Turning to Ernest I asked, "Who should be the next director of the New York State Museum?" His immediate reply was, "You should, of course." I said, "Then write a letter to Carroll Newsom, associate commissioner of state education in Albany, and see what happens. He is in charge of the search." And that is how it all began.

We went on to North Conway, New Hampshire, visiting the Stevenses; Smitty and I had some catching up to do on NRC affairs since his term as chairman was about to expire and he was preparing for his replacement. We all went swimming in a pond loaded with trout that Smitty delighted in showing as we swam underwater. In a day or two we headed for Ragged Mountain to relax with Gene and Sally Magenau.

The Ragged Mountain Club grew out of some Concord, New Hampshire, neighbors who shared a love of the outdoors and built summer cottages on adjacent land; the club was now in its second generation. It afforded tennis, hiking, swimming, trout fishing, and bridge, with an occasional lecture by a member. Buster Norton, a retired school superintendent, was the acknowledged club fisherman. After quizzing me on my skills, and apparently being assured that I used flies only, Buster agreed to take me out on the pond in the morning. He seated me in the stern of one of the club boats and himself at the oars. When he saw me tie on an Ausable Wulf, he remonstrated that New Hampshire brookies favored a Silver Doctor, the only fly he used. When I spotted rises to the far shore, Buster leaned on the oars and said, "Go for it." My Ausable Wulf took enough trout for breakfast.

Returning to duty in September, I had acquired some standing at the NRC. Smitty Stevens, as outgoing chairman of the Division of Anthropology and Psychology, commended me to the president of the National Academy, Detlev Bronk, for my contribution to disaster studies and my representation of the United States at the ICAES the previous summer. The incoming chairman, Harry Shapiro of the American Museum of Natural History, immediately recommended me for a raise in salary. Harry proved a joy to work with.

Staffing at the NRC is not regarded as a career job, but it makes one visible in the national scientific community. I soon received a telegram from Carroll Newsom, associate commissioner of the New York State Department of Education, requesting that I submit a curriculum vitae, a list of publications, and two letters of recommendation if I were interested in becoming a candidate for director of the New York State Museum and Science Service. Until then I had my ears open for a university post, but none of three inquiries had resulted in a solid offer that I could accept.

A week later, a second telegram invited me to come to Albany for a series of interviews on a date specified. I flew to Albany on the appointed day and reported at Newsom's office on the first floor of the State Education Building, at what I later learned was called "Commissioner's Row." Presently I was ushered into Dr. Newsom's presence, and he greeted me with, "We were surprised by your interest. Your name did not appear on any of our lists." Suddenly letters began to arrive, particularly one from Loren Eiseley, whom he had known at Oberlin as a colleague. Newsom, a mathematician trained at Michigan, seemed surprised that I knew Eiseley. After some awkward conversation, he invited me to have lunch at the University Club, a short walk up Washington Avenue. I never felt comfortable in Newsom's presence, then or later. He invariably made one feel that one's accomplishments and colleagues ranked just a shade beneath his own and appeared amazed when they turned out otherwise.

As I was leaving to return to Washington, Newsom said there were two people whom he would ask to review my qualifications: Leslie Spier, a colleague at New Mexico, and Clyde Kluckhohn at Harvard, whom he had come to know in the Southwest. I did not say that Professor Spier had directed my dissertation at Yale, and Kluckhohn, whom I had known for years, and I were planning comparative research on ceremonialism in Iroquoia and the Southwest. I went home assured that they would tell him.

Within a week, Albert Corey, state historian, and John Broughton, principal scientist, geology, descended on Washington to see if I were real. Albert had known me as an assistant professor at Saint Lawrence and was not prepared to accept me as assistant commissioner, a rank to which he aspired; and John, who controlled the biggest share of the Science Service budget, preferred a geologist, possibly himself, rather than another anthropologist. They called at my NRC office, and I phoned Olive, who invited them out to supper and drinks at Turkey Run. While Olive and Bonner rattled pots and pans, the two men faced each other over drinks. They wanted to hear about my trip to London and Cambridge on behalf of disaster studies and my mission to Vienna as delegate to ICAES. Albert responded, "It appears that you are ready." John had no further questions.

I made a third trip to Albany, at Newsom's request. Things were now getting serious. The commissioner of education himself wanted to meet me before a final decision was made on my appointment. Newsom ushered me into the commissioner's baroque office immediately adjacent to the Regent's Room, presented me to the commissioner, and withdrew. Commissioner Wilson had come up the hard way via industrial education from the elementary level and showed the scars of the struggle. He had the reputation of being skilled with politicians and was not above "bellying up to the bar" to advance his budget. He turned to me and said, "I have two questions. First: What do you know about public education in the state of New York? And second: What do you know about geology and related sciences, which are a big part of the museum director's job?"

I told the commissioner that both of my parents had begun as elementary schoolteachers in New York City; that mother had dropped out after marriage but father had risen through the ranks to become dean of Haaren High in Hell's Kitchen; and that I had heard the state system discussed at our dinner table as a youth. I myself was a product of the regents' system through New Rochelle High School, and I was no stranger to it. As an anthropologist, I said, I knew how to do research, I had lived in the community of scientists, both at Smithsonian and NRC, and I knew as much geology as a geologist might be expected to know of anthropology. Moreover, I had learned something about federal funding of research and how to get at it. I could learn how things were done in New York State.

Commissioner Wilson seemed satisfied. He asked no further questions.

A fourth telegram from Dr. Newsom arrived several days later, offering me the position of director of New York State Museum and Science Service, with the possibility of upgrading the position to the assistant-commissioner level, subject to the approval of the Board of Regents. When could I report? I read the message and handed it to Harry Shapiro, who was present. He commented simply, "Congratulations." We agreed that July 1, the start of the federal fiscal year, might be a convenient date. I called Olive and told her we would be moving to Albany. She responded by inviting Harry, who proved a great favorite of hers then and later, to come out for supper.

SIX

The New York State Museum

Leaving spacious quarters on the third floor of the Smithsonian tower for desk space at 2100 Constitution Avenue in 1952 had prepared me for removal to Albany two and a half years later. My research notes, a complete set of the annual reports and bulletins of the BAE, and bound volumes of the *American Anthropologist*, 1937 to date, were shelved in our basement. J. N. B. Hewitt's unbound run of the *American Anthropologist*, 1902–35, and John Swanton's gift of his run of *Journal of American Folklore*, plus my own, were stacked in the coat closet of my NRC office.

Gordon Bowles, son of missionary parents to Japan and a member of Committee on International Relations in Anthropology, came by one day seeking journals for the Christian University of Tokyo Library, which had been burned in an air strike during the 1940s and was being restored. Its staff particularly wanted early volumes of *American Anthropologist*. This struck me as an ideal place for Hewitt's run of the journal, and International Exchanges at SI would arrange to deliver them at no cost to me. I subsequently received glowing letters from Japanese officials promising a fitting reception should I ever visit Tokyo, which, alas, I never did.

As for Swanton's and my back issues of *Journal of American Folklore*, I let a Baltimore bookseller have them in exchange for the reprint edition of the *Jesuit Relations,* which would save me trips to the library whenever I returned to Iroquois research.

On the appointed day—July 1, 1954—I flew to Albany to take up my duties as director of the New York State Museum and Science Service, leaving Olive to cope with packing, the repair of an overflowing septic field, and putting our Turkey Run house on the market. On the airport bus to downtown Albany I met and talked with Norman Rice, then curator, later director, of the Albany Institute of History and Art, with whom I have since had innumerable pleasant encounters. Carroll Newsom had arranged for me to stay at the University Club until I found other digs. He greeted me with a pleasant surprise: my job had been removed from the classified series and upgraded to the nonstatutory rank of assistant commissioner, which meant that I served at the pleasure of the regents of the university. Presently I received a certificate complete with seal and signatures suitable for framing, courtesy of Fred Morse, secretary to the regents. All of this was too much for Arvis Chalmers, columnist for the *Knickerbocker,* who complained that I had been promoted without performing a day's work.

The Albany newspapers printed the announcement of my appointment, which prompted letters from officers of the two leading banks on State Street—the National Commercial Bank and Trust Company and the venerable State Bank of Albany—inviting me to come in for a visit and open an account, which I did. The former bank required row upon row of vice-presidents to do business, whereas the latter got by with a president, two vice-presidents, and a pair of associates. I sat down with one of the senior officers named Hamilton, who accepted my account and helped me over several financial hurdles afterward until he retired. I later learned that he had the reputation of being the hardest-nosed banker in Albany.

Specifications for a house required living space and bedrooms for six people, including Olive's mother, Bonner, not forgetting our Virginia beagle, Oscar, plus stable and pasture for John's horse, to replace Colonel, an army remount character that we left with farmer Marvin Kirby, who stabled him for resale. Bob Kohn, later a leading realtor of commercial property, ransacked Albany, Rensselaer, and Columbia counties in a vain effort to satisfy our requirements and stay within our means.

One morning at breakfast, a resident of the University Club

handed me an ad with a picture of a Greek revival house for sale in North Greenbush, billed as "genuine Colonial." Partial to such architecture ever since my father took me to see the early houses that line the main street of Randolph in southwestern New York, I commented on what style it truly was. Before the day was out I had a call from the realtor: "Would you like to see it?" We arranged to go out late that afternoon.

The property, on north Bloomingrove Drive, Defreestville, recently freed of traffic by Highway 4 from Greenbush north to Troy, comprised several acres and included an old apple orchard to the north of the house and a gully with a trout brook on the south of the drive, leading to a substantial red barn with garage and stables below and haymow above, once accessed by a wagon ramp on the north side. A line of sugar maples led up to the house on the south side, and a row of peonies extended from house to barn on the alternate side. The place had a settled look.

Four Doric columns supported a classic portico and framed the main entrance, although a stoop and door on the driveway-side wing obviously was the way in and out for the occupants.

Other than a cursory look, I pressed the agent not to disturb the owners and retired to the University Club. Next day at the museum office I received a call from the owner, a Mr. Coe, inviting me out for early supper so that I might examine the place before the light faded. He picked me up at four, and during the drive out to Defreestville, I learned that he had followed me at Dartmouth by a decade. He did not say he had been a running back on one of Blackmun's great teams, as I later heard. His employer, a plastic factory in Menands, had transferred him to a plant in another city.

Before dinner I examined the house critically. The roof appeared to be sound, although a cornice showed some sign of deterioration. The formal entrance from the portico opened on a central hallway, from which a staircase, replete with cherry rail and banisters, led upstairs to a second hallway, two north bedrooms, a corridor to a master bedroom and bath, and a stairway to the kitchen entry below. The south wing had been extended to accommodate the master bedroom above and family room below, which featured a fireplace and outside brick chimney midway of the south wall. The kitchen entry door, opening on a stoop and driveway, had become the principal way in and out, leaving the front entrance for formal occasions. Two doors on the left of the staircase opened onto a large space extending across the north end of the house that had been planned as a parlor, which we later divided as study for me and a downstairs bedroom for Bonner.

A single-story wing that might have been the original house extended from the kitchen toward the barn and now afforded a playroom with its own workable fireplace and inside chimney. I walked out to the barn for a second look. The slate roof appeared to be intact: I detected few missing or broken slates. The roof line was straight, which spoke for a firm foundation. And the doors opened and closed readily. The house obviously needed *some* work—but I fell far short of foreseeing how much.

I returned to where Coe and his wife were broiling a steak in an outdoor fireplace. I had made up my mind that the place met our needs and that it had real possibilities. Over a picnic dinner I decided to buy the place. The Coes were amazed and delighted: they had never seen anyone make up his mind so fast. Perhaps it was my early fascination with Greek revival architecture; perhaps it was because the place met our requirements and ended a search in three counties; and perhaps it was simply that as an administrator I liked to solve problems.

That night I reported to Olive what I had done: I had bought the place without her first seeing it. She realized then that we were indeed moving from a house she loved, that she was stuck with making a home in a house she had not seen, and that the whole idea depressed her. Fortunately, neither of us realized that we would be living with carpenters for the next two years.

Reorganizing the Museum

I spent the next two years coping with a budget that had sold the Science Service to the state legislature on the grounds that it conducted applied research that would repay the taxpayers. In fact, most of the scientists were engaged in basic research, which generally yielded knowledge with perhaps long-term applications. My thirteen years at the Smithsonian and my two at the NRC had taught me that applicable results could rest only on a foundation of basic research. In short, the Science Service was justified on a pragmatic fallacy, which I set out to correct. I preached the doctrine of basic research whenever anyone would listen: at budget hearings, at the commissioner's staff meetings, at his retreats, and whenever I was asked to speak or appear on radio or TV.

Perhaps because my predecessor had an ineffectual assistant director, who was counting days till retirement, six museum curators besides the eighteen scientists of the Science Service reported directly to him. I set out to correct this by bringing Victor H. Cahalane, a distinguished mammalogist with field experience in Africa, Alaska, and the American West, from Washington as assistant director and assigning the six curators of collections, exhibits, and school services to him. As for the Science Service, I took the model of the U.S. Geological Survey, heading it with a principal scientist, and created similar surveys for anthropology and biology. Thus I reduced the number of people reporting to me from twenty to four—the heads of the three surveys and the head of the museum. To facilitate communication, these four met with me Monday mornings at ten, keeping each other and me informed. For the entire staff, I held monthly seminars at which I arranged for individual scientists to present some aspect of their research so that others besides myself might hear what they were doing and develop an appreciation of one another. These sessions developed some stimulating feedback from other disciplines.

Since I prepared the budget and defended it within the department, I made an effort to visit field projects of scientists and learn from them what they were trying to accomplish, to enable me to interpret their needs to the department's management personnel who represented us across the street where the state budget was being prepared for the legislature. Interpreting sciences as diverse as paleontology and archeology into "budgetese" was no simple task. Only a few of our research projects had any immediate application.

After two years as director, I decided to make my views explicit by reviving the annual reports of the State Museum, which was approaching its one-hundred-twentieth birthday, and adding the accomplishments of the Science Service. I had learned at Smithsonian how useful such summary reports can be in the scientific community, to administrators of one's host institution, and to individual scientists years later. Although the museum had begun as an independent agency before the mid-nineteenth century, it came under the aegis of the regents of the University of New York during the second half of the century, and not until the early decades of the twentieth did it come under the State Education Department, the operating agency of the regents, created about the time when the Corinthian-columned State Education Building was erected in 1916 on Washington Avenue facing the north entrance of the capitol. The state's natural history and Indian collections occupied the top two floors, and the State Library was accessed by a grand staircase leading from the main lobby to a second-floor rotunda that extended upward to the museum level, reminiscent of the Bibliotheque Nationale in Paris. It was in the library that the card catalog, which had served generations of scholars and students and is fondly remembered today, fell victim of the digital age.

The then state librarian, Charles Francis Gosnell, my colleague and friend during overlapping terms, on seeing my first annual report (Fenton, Research Report, 1958) quipped, "It must be so; it says so on the bottle."

I had barely settled into my job when an outgoing president of Cornell, egged on by a professor of geology and the chairman of the Department of Anthropology, proposed moving the State Museum and Science Service from Albany to Ithaca to a building to be erected on the Cornell campus by the state of New York. Models for such an arrangement already existed on the Cornell campus, and Cornell enjoyed considerable clout in the state legislature. Moreover, Cornell already held several natural-history collections made at state expense during the nineteenth century, which by law should have been deposited in the State Museum.

Not without merit, this proposal generated considerable discussion in Albany: it got the attention of the commissioner and his staff on the first floor; the Albany newspapers ran it; and friends of the museum voiced their affection for the place. My reply took the shape of a blockbuster event featuring some of Albany's cultural treasures.

The Four Kings Exhibit, 1956

While visiting Oxford in the summer of 1952, exploring Blackwood's Bookstore, I had picked up a copy of Richmond P. Bond's *Queen Anne's American Kings*, still warm off the university press. It told the story of three Mohawk men and a Mahican who were taken on a diplomatic mission to London in 1710, feted by fashionable society there, and became known as the "Four Kings." They requested that a missionary be sent to the Mohawks; and after a chapel was built for them at Fort Hunter, New York, in 1711, Queen Anne presented it with a double silver communion set. The set was in use there until the American Revolution, when it was buried for safety's sake (the Mohawks had sided with the British) and later dug up by Mohawks fleeing to Canada. Deseronto's band stayed at the Bay of Quinte with half of the silver, and Joseph Brant's people took the other half to upper Canada, where they settled at Brantford along the Grand River. There they erected a chapel reminiscent of the one at "Indian Castle" on the New York State Thruway, landmarks in both countries, and installed the silver, where I first saw it.

We Fentons, on coming to Albany, had joined the congregation of St. Peter's Episcopal Church, which dates from around the same time—the early eighteenth century. It was the seat of Protestant missionaries to the Mohawks sent out by the Society for the Propagation of the Gospel in Foreign Parts, chartered by Charles II. Among its treasures is a complete set of Francis Garthorne communion silver that Queen Anne commissioned for "Her Majesty's Chapel to the Onondagas," which was never built. The silver first served the garrison and then the communicants at St. Peter's, where it has reposed ever since. It graces the altar Christmas and Easter and may be seen daily just inside the State Street entrance to the church.

After coming to Albany I thought that assembling the Queen Anne silver, with associated material of the period, for the first time since 1712 would make a spectacular exhibit at the State Museum. Charles Gosnell assured me that the State Library held nearly all of the literary material on the Four Kings' visit in London and would join in the venture. After Sunday service, I spoke to Laman Bruner, rector of St. Peter's, and we met that week to discuss my plan and issues such as security and housing for visiting Native councilors. At Ohsweken on Six Nations Reserve, I presented my plan to the elected councilors of the reserve, who were concerned about security, and suggested an RCMP escort to the border, which they would secure. They left it to me to arrange for New York State Police to take them to Albany and protect the silver at the State Museum. I also called on Canon Zimmerman at the Mohawk chapel in Brantford, invited him to participate, and left him to obtain the sanction of the presiding bishop, which was duly granted and signed "Huron," the bishop's title.

Senator H. H. Lehman, former governor of New York, advanced the project by notifying U.S. Customs and Immigration and the Canadian embassy, so that there would be no hitch at the border, either going or returning. He also called the head of the New York State Police. Henri Lehman (who claimed kinship with the senator), curator of ethnology at the Musee de l'Homme, loaned from the Dauphin Collection articles of apparel of the period—moccasins, leggings, a skirt, and so forth—which we put on view under glass bordering the room where the assembled silver went on display. I had succeeded in gathering all but the pieces at Tiyendanega, which proved too complicated to even attempt.

Norman Rice, then curator at the Albany Institute of History and Art, procured the only set of the Simon engravings of the Four Kings yet in Albany from Mrs. Sage of Menands for the library exhibit (now permanent collection of the Albany Institute of History and Art library. Also, Thaw Collection, New York State Historical Association). The Women's Council of the Albany Institute graced the evening of the opening, which guaranteed attendance by a segment of Albany society.

Erastus Corning, who served the longest term of any mayor of Albany during the twentieth century, was a constant friend of the State Museum and a frequent visitor. He graciously loaned the city's portrait of Peter Schuyler, the first mayor, who had accompanied the London visit. I owe many acts of kindness to Mayor Corning. We met one day when he came to view a special exhibit of watercolors by Roy Mason, NA, with whom he shared a love of the outdoors, and I was told he was in the museum. Thereafter, he frequently called me on some related Indian matter.

Three Six Nations councilors and Canon Zimmerman, having arrived and been lodged at St. Peter's parish, delivered their portion of the silver, which they installed in a vacant case next to the one holding the full set from St. Peter's (Fenton, Research Report, 1958). That afternoon Governor Harriman and staff crossed the street to the State Library rotunda, where Commissioner James Allen and I greeted them. I introduced him to the three Iroquois councilors, and since George Buck wore native *gastoweh*[1] and beaded costume, I asked him to give the opening address appropriate to such occasions. I thought the governor and commissioner should hear some native Cayuga. Knowing the content of the speech, called *ganonyonk*, which acknowledges all the blessings the Creator left from earth to sky, I glossed the address, for which act a language specialist in attendance complimented me.

The governor was not amused. He chided me that the exhibit coincided with an anniversary of neither the four native sons' visit to London (1710) nor the arrival of the Queen's beneficence to her majesty's chapels (1712). I had staged the exhibit to honor the International Congress of Anthropology and Ethnology, which was meeting in the United States for the first time that September (1956), and it coincided with International Museum Week of UNESCO, which should have interested Governor Harriman. He did not attend the evening reception.

Toward a New Home for the Museum

The Museum and Science Service badly needed a building designed to accommodate its collections, exhibits, and the research of its scientists. I never made my goal explicit, but I resolved to create the circumstances that would call for a new building. Among the steps my staff and I took were to improve the museum in ways that would attract larger audiences and to raise its profile with the powers that were. It took ten years to get the go-ahead.

Toward attracting more visitors, Assistant Director Victor Cahalane, after surveying museums nationwide, began a program of renovating old exhibits and creating new ones. He moved the mastodons from the rotunda area to the east end of Paleontology Hall, creating a space in which to orient school groups with summary exhibits of various halls. We commissioned a local artist to expand an original watercolor of the Catskills at the end of the Pleistocene, which had been donated by Roy Mason, into the largest mural in Albany.

In addition, after visiting other laboratories in museums, universities, and federal institutions, I convinced a committee that was allocating space in a new wing planned for our present building to devote a whole floor to offices and labs for the Science Service. (As my grandfather used to say, "If your town is run by a committee, be on it.") The new ninth floor connected via a bridge to the museum at the back of Biology Hall. This move freed space in the museum for the curators and the systematic collections in their charge (Fenton, Research Report, 1958).

Renovating the exhibits had an inevitable effect on attendance.

Numbers of both visiting school groups and the general public rose sharply, highlighting the disadvantage of our location. Visitors' origins extended from Monroe County (Rochester) to the Hudson valley and all of Long Island and on to the North Country to the Canadian border (Fenton, Research Report, 1959). Parking for school buses on Washington Avenue became increasingly difficult. I appealed to Mayor Corning to expand the space allotted to school buses. He listened and said, "I'll take care of that." Next morning, all the meters wore hoods west to Eagle Street, and there was consternation along Commissioner's Row among second- and third-level commissioners who regularly parked on the street and sent their secretaries out to "nickel" the meters.

Meanwhile, I continued to try to impress upon the commissioner and other authorities the importance of the museum's role in the state. At the commissioner's 1957 staff retreat at Cooperstown, I spelled out the goals and aspirations of the Museum and Science Service, namely the increase of useful knowledge, the preservation of New York's cultural heritage, and interpretation for the public. For the first time I found acceptance of the fact that both the Museum and the Science Service were indeed engaged in the background variety of basic research in the natural sciences. Research grants from private and national foundations amounting to forty-two thousand dollars in a two-year period affirmed the research policy I had brought to Albany. The commissioner remarked on it, and the money managers of the department took notice (Fenton, Research Report, 1959).

We also got help from the reputation of the Graduate Student Honorarium Program, which the Museum and Science Service had operated for a decade. In the summer months, we employed faculty and graduate students of neighboring universities in field research in areas in which we had some competence. I made a concerted effort to strengthen this program because it kept our staff alive intellectually. I corresponded with and visited the graduate faculties who sent us students. These professors universally acclaimed the program as our best effort. Of the some one hundred alumni of the program up to 1958, many were already teaching, and others made careers in research in areas begun in the program.

I did not lose contact with Harry Shapiro of the American Museum of Natural History, who served a term on the State Museum

Advisory Council along with Vincent Schaeffer of Schenectady, who had known the museum from childhood, before he became famous for seeding clouds at GE Research Labs. Both of these men were of immense help. The Advisory Council recommended the creation of the Commissioner's Committee on Museum Resources, the goal of which was to guarantee a certain level of museum service to every citizen of the state, after the model of State Aid to Libraries. The committee developed a working definition of museum and developed criteria for allocating state aid to museums. Chairman Harold K. Hochschild presented the committee's report to the regents at their meeting on June 29, 1962.[2] The report greatly enhanced the leadership role of the State Museum.

By the time I got an opportunity to make a case for a new museum building—directly to the governor—Commissioner's Row had danced to musical chairs. James Allen came from Harvard as commissioner; Carol Newsom, unsuccessful candidate, departed. E. B. "Jo" Nyquist rose rapidly from assistant commissioner to associate, replacing Newsom, and then to deputy commissioner with direct access to the commissioner and the regents. Hugh Flick became the first associate commissioner for cultural education, to whom I reported directly. Hugh had grown up in the department during his father, Alexander Flick's long reign as state historian and was beloved from basement to topside.

Edward Warburg joined the Board of Regents and immediately chaired the Committee on Cultural Education. The Warburgs, through their foundations, funded philanthropies on an international scale, and Eddie had been active with Nelson Rockefeller in setting up the Museum of Modern Art. Hugh Flick brought him to meet me on his first visit to the department, which afforded me an opportunity to outline our aspirations for a new State Museum.

Within a week of Eddie's visit, Jo Nyquist summoned me to his office to tell me that Chancellor Couper of the regents and Jim Allen, commissioner, had an appointment with Governor Rockefeller to discuss building a new State Museum. "I want you to go with them and present the case, since you know the need and the resources better than anyone." Jo thought it amusing to see whether Rockefeller would recognize his old Dartmouth classmate.

On the day appointed for our meeting with Governor Rockefeller, I had breakfast with Chancellor Couper, Regent

Warburg, Commissioner Allen, and Hugh Flick at their hotel in mid-Manhattan, after which we walked to the governor's New York office, in a row house in the mid-fifties (the Rockefellers owned the whole block). There the heads of the South Mall project preceded us and were in session with the governor. We were ushered into their presence and sat to their right, facing the governor. Couper spoke first and introduced Warburg and Allen, who designated me to present the case for a new State Museum.

The governor replied that he and I needed no introduction, we were old friends, and although he had not visited the present State Museum, he was not unaware of it (his wife, Mary Todd, had told him of her visit). I began by telling what we had learned from a national survey of museums: that the ideal situation called for a site near the junction of the Thruway and Northway adjacent to the university, where there was ample parking, since museum visitors traveled to Albany by car, and where the staff could associate with the university faculty.

The governor stopped me by saying, "That is beside the point. If you want a new museum, it shall be located in the South Mall. Tell me about it." Wallace K. Harrison, architect to the Rockefeller family and in charge of designing buildings in the South Mall, cut in: "Parking is not a consideration; visitors walk to museums."

I resumed by describing the museum's rich holdings in invertebrate paleontology and the Morgan collection of Iroquois arts and material culture, which the regents had commissioned in the 1850s. As I talked I could see the face of Norm Hurd, director of the budget, sometime regent, and aspiring right hand of the governor, getting redder by the minute. General Schuyler, head of the South Mall project, burst in: "A museum is not in the budget."

"Never mind," the governor replied, "We'll find the money. What else is in the State Education Building that needs attention?" Turning to Hugh Flick, I asked his assent to describe the situation at the State Library, which had run out of stack space and needed a modern facility. Hugh nodded, and I explained how, after a fire in 1911 had consumed books and manuscripts, the state librarian at the time, R. W. G. Vail, had scouted the world market and replaced sources on New York and the northeast for a great research library. I mentioned several of its rarities, notably the Cramoisy imprints of the seventeenth-century *Jesuit Relations*.

My instructions from Jo Nyquist were to back off when we had

400,000 square feet of space. By noon we had reached twice that footage, a new museum, and a new library. The project called for a budget of $50 million; it ultimately cost twice that amount.

Brazil, 1954

Herbert Baldus, an expatriate living in Brazil who had attended both the Americanist Congress in Cambridge and the ICAES in Vienna 1952, conscripted a number of us to attend as guests of Brazil a biennial meeting of Americanists in Sao Paulo in the summer of 1954. We had just settled in Albany, New York, but the round-trip ticket I received departed from Albany, Georgia. I appealed to Wallace Atwood, International Relations NAS–NRC, for credentials and help in getting a visa to Brazil. Wally came back and advised that it would be simpler to pick up the visa in Miami, but he would issue a certificate of identity with NRC, with seal and ribbon attached.

In Miami I met up with a New York delegation from Columbia and the American Museum of Natural History, headed by Charles Wagley, who spoke Portuguese, which proved useful later. The Brazilian consulate appeared to be in disorder: they could do nothing for me; I showed my special passport, still valid from Vienna, and the certificate from the NAS–NRC. I was told to go back to my lodging and wait. At midnight someone banged on the door. It was the man from the consulate, still angry. I had put them to much trouble on short notice. But he had the visa in hand, which he finally gave me. We would learn two days later why the Miami consulate was in confusion.

We took off from Miami for the long flight to Rio, via Belem at the mouth of the Amazon. On the flight, Mel Herskovits distributed chapters of a dissertation by his visiting student at Northwestern, a native of Sao Paulo, to prepare us to sit as a committee at the student's dissertation defense. On landing in Belem, our plane was seized by authorities, pending the outcome of the revolution that was in progress. All we learned was that President Vargas had committed suicide. We did not know how long we would be stranded, although the fact explained the turmoil in Miami.

How does one fill the hours while awaiting the outcome of a Latin revolution? Belem has an ethnographic museum, the Museo Goldi, which has a fine collection from the Amazon region. We also visited the zoo. At one stop, I recognized a man from our plane, who said that he was returning from a meteorological conference in Washington, sponsored by NAS–NRC. He had the last room in the hotel. I remarked that we all needed showers, and he arranged for us singly to use the facilities in his quarters, where we lined up and tipped room service for linen.

Meanwhile, Wagley was on the phone with his wife's relatives in Rio. The revolution would be brief, and the chances that the congress would go forward were excellent. Our incoming plane had been commandeered. Another plane was being sent for us.

We went out to the airport to wait. After a night's vigil on hard benches, and little sleep, a new Convair came to carry us to Rio. Evidently we were still guests of Brazil.

Rooms were available for us at a hotel on the plaza, where the U.S. consul advised us to stay indoors until further notice. Next morning the plaza was filled by mounted troops who resembled Native Americans. Revolution or not, the defense of the dissertation would go forward. Four generations of the candidate's relatives braved the streets to sit out the young man's ordeal. They had brought all manner of food and drinks. The candidate's grandfather sat by a tub of champagne. Fortunately, the candidate answered all of the questions satisfactorily, and we all sat down to a feast. Of many such defenses that I have attended, none compares with Northwestern's in Sao Paulo for style.

Confined to quarters for several days, we spent hours in the bar, talking with colleagues before the congress opened. I actually wrote a paper. I came to know Thor Heyerdahl, of *Kon-Tiki* fame, who offered me a place on his upcoming Easter Island expedition. I declined, having barely started in my new post in Albany.

My attempt to cope with elemental Portuguese produced a now amusing incident. On the flight down I had worn a tropical suit that by that time needed cleaning. I gave it to the hotel porter, showed him the tags that read "dry clean only," which I thought he understood, and put the suit in his hands. Next day he returned the suit all smiles. It was beautifully clean. They had washed it, and taken all the gimp out of it. I envisioned a riverbank with favorite rocks where he and his wife had pounded it. I wore the shapeless suit. I must say it was comfortable.

With the all clear, we were free to roam the city. In the evening a bus took us over washed-out roads into the country north of the city, where a steak roast was held in our honor. A long bricked-up grill, waist high to chefs on either side attending steaks, conformed to the slope of the lawn. The long fire afforded the only illumination. The brisk temperature and brilliant night sky reminded me of August in the Adirondacks. I caught my first glimpse of the Southern Cross. While I stood stargazing, Father Martin Gusinde,[3] Austrian ethnologist of *Die Feuerland-Indianer* fame, emerged from the crowd and stood by me shivering. I handed him my raincoat, which he put on, remarking "Bless you. Now go find a warm girl to get next to."

I left next day for the long flight home.

ICAES, 1956: Russians and Indians

I had barely arrived home and prepared my first budget for the State Museum and Science Service when plans for another congress demanded attention. I had carried with me to Albany my official duties as executive secretary for anthropology of the International Congress of Anthropological and Ethnological Sciences, which I had begun at the NRC. During a planning session for the 1956 congress, to be held at Philadelphia, Mel Herskovits suggested that because the Russians were expected to send a delegation, we should invite an Iroquois delegation. The Indians might fulfill the Russians' concern with L. H. Morgan's theory of cultural evolution, which was based largely on Iroquois data. It was up to me to invite them. Knowing that Howard Skye at Six Nations would enlist a strong troupe, I visited him, and he gave me his word, which I knew I could depend on.

During the conference, conversations between Russian delegates and visiting Iroquois produced some amusing incidents. At breakfast, a Russian delegate, mindful of Morgan's stages of cultural evolution—from barbarism to civilization—asked an Iroquois whether they had the plow? The puzzled informant replied, "Yes, but we gave up plows long ago for tractors, which our women and children drive." Farming is a thing of the past at Six Nations.

The University Museum at the University of Pennsylvania has a group of Iroquois False Faces that were collected during the nineteenth century. I showed them to Howard Sky, Deskaheh, and George Buck, who thought they should properly be fed after a century of neglect. The museum backs up on the track and field of the famous Penn relays, where Ted Kidder and I arranged for the Iroquois to demonstrate native games: hoop and javelin, lacrosse, and spear throwing with the index finger in the atlatl mode, as in Snowsnake. Howard had brought a bag of native tobacco *(Nicotiana rustica)*, which he handed to Deskaheh for the invocation. He directed that a fire be kindled on the fifty-yard line, where Deskheh stood waiting for the flames to burn down to embers, when he began the long invocation to the Faces of the Forest, committing a pinch of tobacco for each item mentioned. As if in response to the rising smoke, a great black cloud loomed over the stadium and the Thunders added their rumbling voices. A downpour followed. People ran for cover. I walked behind Deskaheh and George Buck, rain dripping from their feathers, to hear George remonstrate to the old headman in his native Cayuga: "You put too much tobacco in the fire."

Ted Kidder had a bright idea. Our European colleagues had brought dark wool suits, proper dress for a congress in Europe. Philadelphia in early September can be mighty warm. Ted called a local brewery, explained our predicament, and asked about the price of a tractor-trailer load of their best lager. The brewery official replied that the company had supplied beer to all manner of charitable causes but had never before given to science. Why not? The Egyptian hall of the museum was transformed into a beer garden as the brewery truck backed up to the loading dock. It saved the congress.

My participation in affairs of the permanent council slacked off as I settled into my duties in Albany. I did not attend the Paris congress of 1960. The social anthropologists of Britain were not content to leave matters to the permanent council meeting in Prague 1962 but invited its members to meet at the University of London in March of the previous year, offering as an inducement a program of lectures by prominent social anthropologists. I do not recall any substantial business of the permanent council that was transacted, but the lectures were memorable for the circumstances attending their presentation. A blanket of wet snow covered Britain the morning we convened. The authorities, helpless to cope with an emergency that was far worse in the country, hoped that the weather would moderate next day for the queen's anniversary trouping of the horse guards. I walked through slush from my nearby hotel to the university, looking forward to the warmth of the lecture hall. But I was greeted by open windows and colleagues wearing mufflers. An "electric fire" placed near the lectern enabled the speaker to turn pages while the audience weathered the outside temperature just above the freezing mark. Fortunately, I wore a warm suit and kept my topcoat on.

At noon Tom McFeat (Toronto) rallied the troops and announced that we were all going to his favorite pub, the Magpie's Nest. We headed for the financial district and found the nest filled with chaps in dark gray suits wearing bowlers. Tom spoke to the manager, who remembered Tom from the war years and cleared a space for his friends.

Another morning we assembled at Marlboro Palace, near Buckingham, where a member of the royal family would greet us. While waiting, McFeat engaged in conversation with an attractive Yugoslavian physical anthropologist in our midst. In profile she presented the classic straight line from forehead to the tip of her nose, reminiscent of the faces on Greek coins. But the royals, it turned out, were otherwise engaged that day, and none appeared. We drifted back to the university.

British Airways assessed me a substantial fine for the overweight briefcase I carried, full of mimeographed copies of lectures presented at the conference, which I probably never read.

ICOM and ICAES, 1962

In the early summer of 1962, Olive and I flew to the Netherlands to attend the annual meeting of the International Council of Museums (ICOM), which met in The Hague. After the meetings, which directors of museums in Europe regularly attended, I planned to study old collections from North America in the museums of northern Europe and then to visit Prague, where, during the first week of August, the permanent council would review the program proposed for the congress of 1964, which was to be held in Moscow.

Harold K. Hochschild made the former possible, with the charge to visit Tivoli in Copenhagen and Skansen, an outdoor folk museum, in Sweden; a grant from Wenner-Gren covered the Prague meetings. Our ICOM badges served as passports wherever we went.

We visited museums in nine countries: the Netherlands, Denmark, Sweden, Norway, Germany, Austria, Czechoslovakia, Switzerland, and France. In Frankfurt am Main, a pleasant surprise awaited us at the Museum of Ethnology. The curator who greeted us, Dr. Karin Hahn-Hissink, had been sent to Washington around 1947 as one of a hundred German women who were destined to experience American culture by doing housework in selected American homes. While waiting her assignment, Dr. Karin Hahn-Hissink called at my office in the brownstone castle of the Smithsonian, knowing of my participation in ICAES. I called the State Department, reached the person in charge of the German women, and informed that official that Dr. Hahn-Hissink was an esteemed colleague and it would be inappropriate to assign an officer of the Frobenius Institute to housework. It would look better and advance our future relations to enable her to see American collections, visit and talk with colleagues at museums in the United States, and recycle her impressions on returning to Frankfurt. I volunteered to help her select sites and plan an itinerary. This we did.

The scholar whom I rescued from housework fifteen years previously in Washington went out of her way to return the favor. Dr. Hahn-Hissink provided me with an assistant to retrieve and photograph the few Iroquois specimens in the collection, all undocumented. They took particular pride in a mask of the Niagara Falls style, which I regard as the type specimen of this genre (Fenton, *False Faces*, 1987). I would soon learn that European collections were largely undocumented, save with the name of the collector, dealer, and an accession date.

Having exhausted the collections at Frankfurt in a morning, Dr. Hahn-Hissink telephoned colleagues in neighboring museums and at Heidelberg University, arranging appointments. She assigned a graduate student named Lindig to drive us there and interpret, if need arose. Lindig, a former U-boat junior officer, had learned English as a prisoner of war in maritime Canada. He proved a good companion and knew his way around.

Hahn-Hissink and Lindig were both eager for us to see the Speyer collection, which numbered several rare items that were alleged to have been tossed from the windows of the Berlin ethnographic museum to private scouts following an air raid. After several attempts, word came that Arthur Speyer would receive us, and Lindig drove us there.

It was going on four o'clock when we arrived, and Speyer greeted us at the door. The aroma of coffee reached us from within. Speyer seated me at a table of covered objects; Olive sat in an adjacent room with women and family. We had not anticipated being admitted to a middle-class German home. Speyer asked about my mission. When I assured him that I was a scholar, not a collector, seeking objects of Native American origin that had found their way to Europe, he relaxed somewhat and admitted to having seen some of my publications.

The first object he uncovered was a False Face in the Grand River style that I dated from the first or second decade of the twentieth century, though he regarded it as much older and valued it at an exorbitant price. His other treasures were comparable.

Back in Frankfurt, Karin Hahn-Hissink had planned dinner for us at home. We arrived at the appointed hour in a residential area of some standing: great shade trees resembling American basswoods, but badly scarred or missing whole sections from bombing during the war. Our hostess's house had taken a direct hit, but she entertained us handsomely in the section still standing.

I recently contacted Christian Feest, now director of the Museum of Ethnology Vienna, but formerly the leading Americanist at Johann-Wolfgang-Goethe-Universität in Frankfurt, to bring me up to date on people who had assisted us in Frankfurt. He replied, "Sad to say, Karin Hahn-Hissink . . . passed away several years ago (and left the Frobenius Institute her substantial wealth)." He reminded me that Hahn-Hissink had come from a wealthy Dutch family, held a doctorate in anthropology, and had done interesting fieldwork in Bolivia. Feest continued: "Lindig, my predecessor, . . . after he retired, let his hair grow long and became a painter (and dropped out of anthropological circles). I saw Arthur Speyer about ten days ago. At age 80, he is of course a youngster, relatively speaking" (Christian Feest, personal communication, September 8, 2002.)

At the Municipal Museum in Mannheim I studied and photographed two fine wampum belts, both of eighteenth-century origin I judged, but without documentation. In Hamburg, I found nothing of significance in the ethnology museum. Olive, meanwhile, attempted to dine in a restaurant near our hotel. In her best Syracuse German, she ordered from the menu what she assumed was chicken. What the waiter served was a plate of chicken necks. When I returned to the hotel I found her in a deep case of culture shock. Just then the telephone rang. It was Mrs. Warburg telling us that cousin Eddie had called from New York; would we come out to the house for supper? They were going sailing and afterward would be by at four to pick us up. We both took naps.

We were downstairs at the appointed hour when a Mercedes drove up to the door. The driver, dressed in "whites," introduced himself as Mr. Warburg and, to make room for us, proceeded to move the lines and gear that sailors inevitably carry. We were soon comfortably seated and on our way to the Warburg estate at Blankenese, some miles northwest of Hamburg.

Our hosts had dismissed the servants for the day, but they served us drinks and we four relaxed while I explained how Eddie and I had come to know each other. Presently Mr. Warburg took us on a tour of the house while his wife retired to the kitchen to fix supper. The most memorable feature of the tour was a huge room, cleared of furniture, now containing a dozen cots, each covered with blankets, a towel, washcloth, and bar of soap for the nearby showers. The main living room had been converted to a dormitory for refugees from the East Zone passing west to freedom. Just then the room was empty. Mr. Warburg told us that the flow had diminished of late.

After a simple supper, Mr. Warburg drove us to a nearby train station, bought our tickets back to Hamburg, instructed the stationmaster to tell the conductor where to put us off, and handed me the pair of tickets. Presently an ancient steam engine belching brown smoke and hauling a train of ancient coaches came to a stop where we stood waiting. We boarded and were soon in Hamburg within a short walk to our hotel. Hamburg ended on a happy note.

We flew north to Copenhagen Monday morning and booked in at a small hotel. Our first obligation was to fulfill Harold Hochschild's charge to visit Tivoli Gardens at night. The gardens were indeed spectacular, and the rides somehow fit in and did not seem out of place. I have a vivid impression of two senior Danish women sitting on a nearby bench, both smoking short fat cigars, evidently pleased with themselves and the scene. For scores of Danish families and lovers from every country, Tivoli was a fun place.

Monday morning I commenced a week of productive research at the Danish National Museum while Olive explored the myriad shops for which Copenhagen is famous. The foyer of the museum displayed treasures from the collections: notably two wampum-inlaid war clubs, one of which had lashed at the foot a double-bitted stone adze of a type commonly called a bar celt that occurs sporadically in archeological collections from the Northeast, which explains how bar celts were sometimes used. The two inlaid clubs had been brought from "New Sweden" in the early seventeenth century. The other treasure that caught my eye was a portrait of Henry Abeel, son of Cornplanter, by John Bird King, 1827 (Fenton 1998: 661).

The museum's director, Kaj Birket-Smith, whom I had met at the Americanist meetings in Cambridge, received me in his office, together with two aides. I explained that I particularly wanted to see the Seneca collection that L. H. Morgan had made in 1862 for Count Radloff, which complemented the pieces lost in the New York state capitol fire of 1911 from the collection Morgan had made for the regents a decade earlier. Birket-Smith gave me carte blanche to proceed as I pleased and instructed the aides to give me whatever assistance I needed in opening cases and studying objects. The two women made museum studies a joy: mid-mornings we stopped for coffee, and at noon they wouldn't hear of my going out for lunch, but spread a table with delicate Danish pastries and other edibles; Birket-Smith frequently joined us. One day they invited Olive, unless she were still shopping. The risk, to which most American women succumbed sooner or later, lay in a "short one" or a "long one" (fur coats) or in Danish silverware. Olive did buy a set of table knives with rosewood handles, which I treasure.

The State Ethnographical Museum of Stockholm holds two clubs from New Sweden, of which one is the mate to the double-bitted adze club in Copenhagen—although instead of stone, the adze is of wrought iron forged by some Swedish smith, possibly in the New World. The other collection I studied came from M. R. Harrington's best period of collecting in the first decade of the twentieth century, when he kept field notes; it included three Iroquois wooden False Faces and two finely woven Husk Faces, which I photographed (Fenton, *False Faces*, 1987).

On the advice of our travel agent, we took the day-long canal trip west across Sweden, over connecting glacial lakes with white birch–lined shores, to a point where we could board the train for Goteborg, arriving late that night. Because our flight to Munich left early, we saw little of Goteborg, missing its famed Museum of Ethnology.

The Munich Ethnological Museum yielded nothing to my particular research, which freed me to pursue other interests. Lederhosened natives welcomed us to Munich's famous beer hall, shared a round of drinks with us, and urged us to give voice to the lieder of the moment. We did not return for the roisterous evening. The small hotel where our agent had booked us, mindful that most tourists desired to be close to the beer hall, was but a block away: the racket kept us awake most of the night. Next morning we gathered our luggage and walked to the nearest grand hotel, where we announced that we came as refugees from the Hotel Platzl. The concierge, although the hotel was booked solid, recalled some empty servant's quarters on the roof, which we could examine and, if to our liking, rent at a reasonable price. Olive spotted a clothesline, which at that point in our travels proved an extra amenity. To our delight, Alexander Paar, his wife, and daughter Victoria, whom we had come to know in Scheveningen, Netherlands, and for whom I had contributed to his journal, *Curator* (Fenton 1960), greeted us when we returned to the lobby. Together we shared some of Munich's rich culture.

Olive and I attended an outdoor concert at the Residenz, a former palace, now a lawn within the foundations of a ruined home of Bavarian princes, as we were told by a Fräulein seated next to us who had spent a year at Mount Holyoke College in New England and spoke excellent English. A chamber orchestra gave a program of classics, and a young violinist from east of the Iron Curtain performed a splendid rendering of a famous concerto. I often wonder where his career led him. His performance was one of the highlights of our trip. On the way home, a column of marching veterans of the Afrika Corps forced us off the sidewalk into the road. I complained to the concierge when we reached the hotel, and he said he would notify the police that guests were being harassed. I heard nothing further about this single unpleasant incident.

In browsing shop windows next day, what appeared to be an early map of New Netherland caught my eye. Could this be a restrike of Visscher's map of 1655, or of Van der Donck's map of the following year, from the original plates? Or a clever reproduction from a print? It proved to be an imprint from a copy of Ioachim Otten of Amsterdam's reworking of Visscher, commemorating the Dutch reconquest of New York. The date August 24, 1673, appears in a cartouche; the Dutch takeover occurred on August 9. It shows in great detail the Hudson and Mohawk country. I bought a copy and had it shipped home where it was mounted and framed at the New York State Museum to hang in my office, and now in my Cooperstown study.

From Munich we went briefly to Stuttgart, the scene of heavy industry, where allied bombing had destroyed whole sections of the city, since rebuilt of cement block and poured concrete structures. From Stuttgart we flew to Vienna and checked in at the Imperial Hotel, where Saudis had stayed the previous week. I had wanted Olive to experience the Bristol, where I had stayed ten years earlier, but the Imperial more than made up for it in amenities. Olive had to send for the maid to explain the directions on the tub. Once more her Syracuse German failed her. Annie Hohenwart, an anthropologist and principal assistant to Robert Heine-Geldern at the Institute for Ethnology, next day recalled the Hapsburg balls at the Imperial before World War I. She had made her debut there.

From Vienna we traveled to Prague by rail. A large Czech woman from the Czech equivalent of Intourist met our train and proceeded to sort us out by national delegations and direct us to waiting cabs that drove us to separate hotels. Vinigi Grotanelli, a Roman aristocrat and ethnographer whom I had come to know in Vienna, spotted us and rode to our hotel, which was of recent construction, modest but adequate, and joined us in our room for conversation over drinks. He would join the American delegation next day on a tour of St. Vitus Cathedral and adjacent cultural monuments over the Charles River Bridge. The American delegation to the Permanent Council of ICAES was now complete: Mel Herskovits, chair; A. I. "Pete" Hallowell; Henry Collins; and myself. Vinigi asserted his independence again by going to the altar rail in the cathedral, kneeling, and praying while the rest of us stood by.

The first session of the permanent council meeting in the old Czech Academy of Sciences soon ended on a note of frustration. The Soviet delegation had failed to bring an interpreter familiar with anthropological terms and ethnological concepts, and the interpreter supplied by the Soviet embassy proved inadequate. The French delegation complained strenuously. I asked the archaeologist Andre Leroi-Gourhan, who sat to my right, how he had become so facile in Russian. He replied, "I learned Russian as a boy from the milkman, a White Russian noble who fled to Paris during the Revolution." He had protested that the interpreter was not saying what he heard—in French or in English.

The council reconvened a day later, a fresh interpreter having been flown in from Moscow. The morning passed in disagreements over the agenda. The Soviet members seemed unused to the give and take of the western world. On the third or fourth day I asked Mel Herskovits for permission to try a tactic I had learned in Iroquois councils—to break a major proposition into small parts, advance them over several days, and get agreement on the parts, until the concept emerged full blown. Meanwhile, the council might resume arguing. First, I addressed the presiding Russian chair, saying that I understood that they were interested in L. H. Morgan, whom we regarded as the founder of social anthropology. This he acknowledged. I left it there. The second day, I again addressed the chair to say that some of us would like to hear the Russians' views on Morgan, and we would share ours. The third morning, I again interrupted the discussion to add that a symposium on the theory and accomplishments of Morgan seemed appropriate for the congress. Professor Oderagge remarked, "We thought of that. But if we proposed it, it would be regarded as propaganda; but since you propose it, it is science." The fourth day, Professor Oderagge turned to me and announced: "Our committee has met and approved your suggestion."

At the close of the third day, Alfred Métraux came by to say, "People are wondering where you learned diplomacy?" I answered, "Tell them in the Tonawanda woods, from the old Seneca sachems."

Having set the theme of the congress, which the Russians scheduled as the opening plenary session at Moscow, I had made my contribution and was ready to resume research in Swiss collections. And Olive and I were concerned just then about our need to communicate home: our daughter, Betsey, was about to reach term with her second child. We decided to catch the next flight to Zurich, the nearest point west of the Iron Curtain.

During the hour's flight from Prague to Zurich, the plane leveled at perhaps twenty-five thousand feet, affording a view of the landscape below. Instead of the usual patchwork of small cultivated fields, the land had been stripped of trees until it resembled a barren wilderness as we approached the Iron Curtain. Once past the grim watchtowers, fields were lush and green.

In Zurich we were booked into the Carleton Hotel, a first-class establishment owned and operated by the Ritz family of Paris, a marked contrast to our meager, Communist-run quarters in Prague. The concierge was most helpful in arranging trans-Atlantic calls home, which reassured us that Betsey was thriving. After a boat tour down Lake Zurich, I was ready to start looking at collections.

The University of Zurich's ethnological collection yielded a fine example of a braided and coiled Husk Face (Fenton, *False Faces*, 1987). From the lake, the main street of Zurich stretched north to the railroad station and was suitably named Bahnhofstrasse. Midway, a department store had devoted its street windows to scenes of the customs and usages of the Swiss people. There, for my benefit, were the analogs and parallels to the Iroquois False Faces that I knew so well.

The largest collection of Swiss masks available for study was housed at the Rietberg Museum, a former lakeside villa where Brahms resided and composed for some years, now owned by the municipality. I spent the morning examining the masks and their correspondence to Iroquois False Faces, but in a unique style. There are only a limited number of ways in which a human face can be portrayed; there are bound to be parallels that are not culturally related.

In the early 1960s, a Swiss schoolteacher from Zurich named Hoz and his wife came to the New York State Museum to view the Morgan collection and related material. Hoz had read my article on the False Faces of the Iroquois in the 1940 Annual Report of the Smithsonian Institution (Fenton 1941). He told me about his personal collection, which I was eager to see. Meanwhile, Hoz had retired and sold the collection to the Zurich municipality, which assigned it to the Kunz Gewerbeschule (School for Applied Art), where I went to see it. I was told that the collection was not available for study—that it was presently stored in a sub-basement. I protested that I had come a long way to see it, that I preferred to study it in storage rather than on exhibit, and that I did not mind working alone in a sub-basement. They were evidently embarrassed for an American to know that the facility had been designed as an air-raid shelter in a more dangerous era. An elevator used for upper floors reached the facility, and it was air conditioned. I proceeded happily to examine and photograph three Iroquois False Face masks of moderate age and other interesting pieces.

Done with Zurich, which we greatly enjoyed, we rode Swiss Rail to Basel on the Rhine, discovering for the first time the joys of trains arriving on time and departing on the minute. The ethnological museum in Basel ranks among the best in Europe, having fine African and Melanesian collections and exhibits, though only a box of moccasins brought home from eastern Canada by Swiss tourists. I had a long talk with the director, who had not attended the Prague meetings and was eager to hear how it had come out. I predicted that the Russians would be reasonable.

Our grand European trip of 1962 wrapped up with stops in Bern and Geneva. The Bern Historical Museum held two nineteenth-century collections from the Great Lakes area of Canada, both of which contained some fine pieces. One was attributed to Captain Malcolm, Montreal 1828; the other represented the dress and paraphernalia of a stranded troop of "Indians abroad" abandoned in Bern, who sold all but their breechclouts to raise passage home.

In Geneva, the curator of the ethnological museum produced a lone Iroquois False Face, which I judged to be of mid-nineteenth-century derivation. More interestingly, Olive and I sought out Bert and Stella Lesch Deignan, had drinks at their apartment, and reminisced about the Smithsonian and Washington, which we had shared for a dozen years. After dinner at a very good restaurant, Bert and I sat on the beach for an hour. I tried to get Bert to tell me about the ill-fated Mountford Australian expedition, for which I had been slated while at the BAE, only to have Assistant Secretary Alex Wetmore replace me with Frank Setzler, whom Wetmore had elevated to head curator, thereby creating an uproar. Bert preferred not to talk about it, beyond saying that I was lucky to have stayed home.

We caught a flight to Paris, lodged overnight, and next morning took the boat train to Brest, where we boarded the *Queen Mary* for New York. She was a noble ship. I watched the Brest electric crane operators loading autos into the forward hold. They would, on signal, snatch a car from dockside, line it up with the hatch, and drop it precipitously into the hold without touching the sides of the hatch, braking it just short of the keel. Such operating skill suggested long years of learning. Tourist accommodations were in the stern of the ship behind first class. Two days out, a north Atlantic storm raised a high sea. Periodically the propellers surfaced, causing the whole stern to shake. We weathered the storm without missing a meal.

On August 19, a radiogram announced the birth of Alexandra Lyle to Betsey in Tampa, Florida, to our great relief. Her older brother nicknamed her Zama, her name ever since.

Moscow 1964: Morgan Revisited

My participation in the Eighth International Congress of Anthropological and Ethnological Sciences, held in Moscow on August 3–10, 1964, represented the climax of my involvement in these congresses, which had begun in 1952. Because I have published two accounts of American involvement in the Moscow congress, I shall confine myself here to some amusing incidents in which I was involved that are not already in print.[4]

It was the last summer of Khrushchev's term, and the Russians were on their good behavior. They very much wanted the congress to succeed. The atmosphere was correct and cordial. The congress was attended by 1,094 delegates who represented fifty-eight countries and presented papers in twenty-seven sections, totaling 812 communications, besides several plenary sessions held in the great hall of Moscow University. The American delegation numbered well over one hundred, not counting spouses and children, which an English colleague characterized as a veritable invasion. Ted Kidder and I shared leadership of the American contingent, and he asked me to represent us at the opening session, since I had attended the Prague meeting of the permanent council two years previously and had proposed the symposium on L. H. Morgan that was scheduled for the second day. He would represent us at the U.S. embassy, where his brother was posted.

I reported at the presidium of the great hall at the appointed time and was ushered into a reception room directly behind it. A long table with rounded ends spanned the length of the room, dressed with individual place settings, each affording a bottle of water, a glass for vodka, a second-grade apple, and tableware. One stood to partake, for the chairs lined the walls. I sat down on the left. Various persons strolled in, exchanged greetings with a man standing at the head of the table, whom I was told represented the Kremlin and would open the congress, and passed on the far side of the table to gather at the remote end, as far as possible from the locus of power. The Kremlin representative wore an immaculate silver-grey tailored jacket with choke collar and matched trousers, not unlike the uniforms worn by chauffeurs to Park Avenue residents of the 1920s.

Presently Gregulevic, a Georgian physical anthropologist whom I had met in Prague, wandered in and spoke longer with the Kremlin representative, turning my way. Not knowing Russian, I inquired of the Kremlin representative afterward in fractured French, "What did he say?" I had guessed right: French, the prestige language of the old regime, was still cultivated. He replied, "He warned me to watch out for you on two accounts: first, you don't smoke, and second, you learned diplomacy from savages."

The congress met a second day in plenary session to hear the Morgan symposium, which initiated the scientific sections of the meeting. The first speaker, a woman sociologist of Boston University named Constas, whose work I did not know, delivered a scathing indictment of Marxist interpretations of Morgan's theories, which set the audience's teeth on edge. She may have been right, but it was a poor start. As second speaker, I faced a hostile audience. Once more I resorted to "forest diplomacy." I had brought photographs of surviving objects of material culture that Morgan had collected, now in the New York State Museum. I called upon a curator of some appropriate museum to come forward to the podium and accept them.

After some hesitation, a woman curator advanced up the aisle and I handed the photographs to her, a gesture that pleased the audience. Then I proceeded to my own paper, which projected the theory that Morgan developed in *Ancient Society* (1877) to recent political developments among the descendents of the Iroquois whom Morgan studied.[5] The piece was well received. To quote one Russian colleague: "It was weak on theory, but you gave us new information. You brought Morgan up to date. Second, you did not attack the Marxists, so we did not have to defend them; and third, you finished on time."

As I walked down the center aisle of the great hall, Margaret Mead stepped out to embrace me, saying, "That was lovely, Bill. You saved us all from embarrassment."

Family Matters

After Turkey Run, Olive never liked the house and barn that I had bought unseen by her in North Greenbush. For two years she lived with workmen, notably a "farmish" carpenter named Clarence

Kimmey, who came to us recommended by a local lumber dealer, remodeling the house to fit the needs of our family. She divided the north parlor with a wall to create a downstairs bedroom for her mother, Bonner, and a study for me. I came home one day to discover the south wall of the one-story original kitchen wing open to the elements and propped up by two-by-fours. On asking Clarence what his plans were, he commented, "You can have a garage, or a 'pitcher' window, whichever you decide." I told him to restore the wall.

Under previous owners, the mow floor in the slate-roofed barn had become the local basketball court, and the neighborhood boys assumed the right to use it at their pleasure. When I caught one of the lads smoking and padlocked the doors, our house was stoned at night from the road. I called one parent, who was uncooperative if not hostile, but local farmer Philips brought his son to apologize. The boy later became Betsey's escort at various high-school events. Before that Betsey had complained, "Daddy, no one here knows how to give a party." Things improved after that.

John also entered Columbia High, where he discovered an aptitude for science, but dyslexia slowed his advancement in the social sciences and English. After looking for another school where he could get some help, we settled on the Milne School, run by the Department of Education of the State College at Albany, presently the University at Albany. There his interest in science intensified, and in the logic of Latin grammar he found a basis for English. Moreover, Olive, in interviewing his teachers, found in a Mr. Cochrane someone who taught John the English language with a slip dictionary, with the result that John became a competent writer. In his final year at Milne, an advisor warned us that John was not "college material." Nevertheless, he entered Cornell via the Agriculture College, took liberal arts subjects, and graduated high in his class, having majored in genetics.

Doug, having passed two years in the Langley Cooperative School in Virginia, which his mother had helped organize during the war years when transportation became difficult, entered the Belltop School in North Greenbush to discover that he lacked the requirements of grades one and two. While at Belltop, Doug followed his age mates into Little League. The first year was not a success for Doug, who kept striking out and came home crying in frustration. But the second year, on opening day, Doug hit the first pitch over the flagpole in center field. He kept the ball.

The Northwood School on Lake Placid offered Doug an outlet for his talent in sports—both football and hockey—although with one exception the year was not an academic success. In "Spike" Witherell, retired Norton Company executive of Troy, who had joined his son on the faculty at Northwood, Doug found a tutor who taught him basic mathematics, a subject in which for the first time Doug developed real competence. It later carried over into a career as a manufacturer's representative.

An old apple orchard of overgrown trees covered several acres north of the house and barn, extending to a rough hillside filled with brush and sumac. The boys helped me decide that a pickup truck might satisfy John's urge to drive, inspire him to learn auto mechanics, and help with work around the place. From a used truck dealer in Menands I bought the oldest truck on the lot for one hundred dollars and had it delivered, with no intention of licensing it. We harvested apples, transferred them to our station wagon, and drove to a cider mill near Troy, which bought them worms and all. John lacked the least interest in auto mechanics but loved to drive the truck over an obstacle course through the brush behind the orchard, which contributed to its early demise. Doug and his friend Donny, not to be outdone, although neither could reach the pedals, managed to move the vehicle by means of one of them sitting on the floor and pushing pedals by hand while the other shifted gears and drove. It was an eerie sight.

Last Years at the Museum

While I was gallivanting around Europe seeking old collections from North America, several significant achievements were in the works back home, principally by the scientists in the laboratories secured for them in the annex to the State Education Building. The long-awaited *Geologic Map of New York* (1961), compiled by the staff of the Geological Survey, survived budgetary restrictions, sold out, and soon reappeared in a larger printing. The prehistory of New York and its attendant settlement patterns assumed final shape in the hands of William Ritchie and Robert Funk of the Anthropological Survey. And in biology, Eugene Ogden's work on pollen and its dissemination, and Hugo Jamnback's studies of black flies promised comfort to Yorkers. These scientists merited new laboratories and better equipment.

Once the new State Museum was a certainty, everyone wanted in on the act. The morning after I returned from the audience with Governor Rockefeller, an upwardly mobile representative of the Education Department's office of management called on me to announce his intent to devote himself full-time to advancing the project. After assuring him that major decisions remained in my hands, I accepted his services. He was of immense help in dealing within the department and with other agencies of state government. He later headed his division of the Education Department. From outside I received all manner of inquiries from museologists. In accepting outside advice, I relied on demonstrated skills in their home institutions that I knew—namely, the Royal Ontario Museum at Toronto and the Smithsonian Institution.

Fortunately, Assistant Director Victor Cahalane, who had directed the renovation of exhibits in the old museum, had prepared a prospective program and exhibits for a museum on the Mall, and I had written a parallel statement for the building (Fenton, Research Report, 1963). I had something to show architect Wallace Harrison when he and I sat down over lunch in the education cafeteria and he asked me about the purpose and programs while he sketched on paper napkins renderings of a building he was about to design. After that meeting I dealt with subordinates.

The collection of nineteenth-century furniture, which included an important inventory of Shaker items, had never had a competent curator. I enticed Carroll Lindsay, a specialist in decorative arts at the Smithsonian, to join the staff. Unfortunately, salary scales between the two institutions did not mesh, and the competent assistant director, an empirical scientist, found it discomforting to deal with a flamboyant and ambitious operator who had all of the social graces and who immediately identified with the elite of Albany.

My other mistake in judgment was to employ Duncan Cameron of the Royal Ontario Museum as a consultant. I no longer recall what Duncan contributed beyond some brilliant conversations and immodest fees, but Vic Cahalane retired to my chagrin, and our personal friendship suffered for a year or two. That the whole enterprise would require different personnel from those of us who brought it recognition led me to reconsider how I would spend the rest of my life.

After a decade as assistant commissioner, I knew that I did not want to spend my allotted time in further administration.

Betimes I recalled Edmund Wilson's urging me to write an Iroquois classic, which I could not manage on the job, even though a sabbatical of six months enabled me to complete one chapter on the cosmology for a book contract that Edmund persuaded Roger Strauss to underwrite with a substantial advance. With passing years and no further progress, I returned the advance unspent. Roger proclaimed my gesture, unheard of in his experience, "positively un-American."

Various academic appointments loomed on the horizon. The first luminary showed from Toronto, where I had a longtime association with Thomas F. McIlwraith, who had first befriended me as a graduate student attending my first American Anthropological Association meeting at Andover Academy in 1931. A decade later, during interludes of fieldwork at Six Nations, Tom put me up at Hart House, residence of visitors to the University of Toronto, and introduced me over sherry to his family. Confronting retirement, Tom proposed me as his successor and hosted a grand luncheon presided over by the provost, the incoming minister of the exterior, at which T. F. praised my ability to keep up my personal research while holding an administrative post.

The offer of a professorship at a leading Canadian university and the chairmanship of its department of anthropology honored and tempted me, although I finally declined for several reasons. Meeting my then salary would have required a distinguished chair and subjected me to criticism from Canadian colleagues. And, as Olive remarked, "We are not that mad at President Eisenhower that we have to move to Canada." Further, turmoil within the department far exceeded that in the museum, which I could handle.

Two years later, the vice-president of the university invited me to Toronto to help select a replacement for T. F., at that point deceased, and I was able to recommend Tom McFeat at the National Museum of Man in Ottawa. McFeat was a native son and veteran of World War II, having served in the Canadian Army on the European front. McFeat was appointed and served out his term until retirement. Upon my return to Albany, after a dicey flight in heavy snow, Olive greeted me with the alarming news that son Doug was in Lake Placid Hospital with pneumonia. Next day we drove the 160 miles over winter roads to the north country to learn that Doug was responding to treatment and was out of danger. Dr. Bergamini was a reassuring presence.

I encouraged Thomas Abler to study the history of factionalism and political parties among the Seneca Nation of Indians, using minute books, census records, and extensive documentation in libraries and archives in Philadelphia. Merle Deardorff of Warren, Pennsylvania, and several past presidents of the Nation helped get him started. The Nation council granted permission and opened their records. Abler submitted a part of his study as a dissertation at Toronto, and Tom McFeat asked me to read it as an outsider. I attended the defense of dissertation in Toronto, which the candidate carried off with aplomb. As if in celebration, my flight to Buffalo, this time in sunlight, passed merrily with a troupe rehearsing their evening show. A flight attendant informed me that they were the "Johnny Cash Show," which I did not yet know of. Cash sat far forward and did not participate. I suppose he was equally ignorant of the dissertation rite in which I had just taken part.

A second opportunity came from the State University of New York at Buffalo, where several colleagues whom I had known in Washington during the 1950s had taken root. Haxie Smith and George Trager, both brilliant linguists, were promoting my selection; Trager had preceded me at Taos and liked my piece on factionalism (Fenton 1957). It was worth a visit to assess the prospects of joining them.

Olive, reluctantly, and I drove the 260 miles of Thruway from Albany and exited at Williamsville to lodge at a motel near the university. Buffalo had been a mecca during Olive's girlhood in Salamanca, and I mistakenly assumed that she would welcome living there. Instead, the prospect depressed her. When I asked why, she replied, "I have been to Buffalo." She preferred living in her Slingerlands house where we had been since 1959.

The Haxie Smiths had us home for cocktails and supper with key faculty and wives. Olive remained quiet, answering questions put to her in a matter-of-fact way. Trager and I talked about Taos. We left early and went back to the motel, and Olive cried all night.

The following day proved equally unpromising. After breakfast we were besieged by real-estate agents, women determined to sell us a house. Their first question—"How much do you expect in salary?"—they deemed essential before showing us houses. I replied by describing what we expected to replace our Slingerlands house. Virtually every house we looked at was smaller than our present one, overpriced, and within the shadow of a transmission tower, often with a leg of the tower inside the fence line, transmitting power from Niagara to western New York and beyond. It was a forbidding prospect.

While Olive rested, Haxie and I reviewed course assignments and discussed compensation as he tried to stretch the university pay scale to match my salary as assistant commissioner. We returned home to await further word. I had decided to decline the offer before he called. We had put down deep roots in Slingerlands.

After Sunday service at St. Peter's in Albany, "Van" Collins, long-time president of the State College at Albany, whom I had known at Dartmouth, greeted me. When I asked him what he planned for the new University at Albany, which Governor Rockefeller had commissioned Edward Durell Stone to design on the site of the former Albany Country Club, Van said, "Come see me and I'll tell you."

I went to see Van on the downtown campus of the college on Washington Avenue, where, while Albany slept, Van had converted a first-rate teacher's college into a liberal-arts institution that was on the verge of becoming a university. I told Van that I was seeking to shed administration for an opportunity to complete several research projects while training some graduate students. Further, I would enjoy visiting colleagues nationwide toward recruiting younger faculty for a first-rate anthropology department. Van, who had the reputation of being hard to talk to, listened and remained noncommittal. I came away expecting to hear nothing further.

Presently, one or two faculty members in sociology, themselves anthropologists, called at my State Museum office and joined me for lunch downtown. Walter Zenner, whom I had met at an American Ethnological Society meeting, seemed genuinely interested in my proposal. Paul Wheeler, then dean of social and behavioral sciences, followed and requested a curriculum vitae and a list of publications. Matters were getting serious. If the university met my terms, I was prepared to accept.

I did not have long to wait. Over lunch with Dean Perlmutter of the College of Arts and Sciences, we agreed on the title "research professor of anthropology" at my present salary, subject to later increments, with the expectation that I would pursue my research and recruit younger faculty for a department of anthropology. I found a physical anthropologist at Ann Arbor and an Africanist at UCLA and assisted in bringing a rising generalist from Maine.

I resigned my post as assistant commissioner for the State Museum and Science Service and paid my respects to the commissioner, who invited me to meet with the regents; he spoke of research accomplished under my direction, and I told them what I hoped to achieve in the future. I began my long association with the State University of New York at Albany as of January 1, 1968, unaware that I would complete a third term of thirteen years, which would complete my official career.

19. Bill and Olive, engaged, in 1935.

20. Bruce Fenton at Alfred University, 1936.

21. Christmas at Turkey Run, 1946.

22. Jim Skye and Bill with award for teaching Cayuga, given by the State University at Albany, 1978.

23. Bill in his Slingerlands study, 1989.

24. Harold Conklin (*left*), Bill's sponsor for the Wilbur Cross Medal, and Bill, 1999.

25. Presentation of the Wilbur Lucius Cross Medal for Distinguished Alumni of the Yale Graduate School, 1999.

26. Maxine Crouse Dowler and Bill with beadwork frame at celebration in Cooperstown, October 2003.

SEVEN

Research Professorship at Albany

My first priority as research professor at SUNY Albany was to prepare a copy of Father J. F. Lafitau's "Customs of the Indians," which I had begun with Elizabeth Moore in 1939, for the editors of the Champlain Society of Toronto. The project had advanced by fits and starts over the years, as each of us was involved in tasks of higher priority. Moore completed the translation early on and ran down Lafitau's sources in the Bibliotheque Nationale, and after I moved to Albany, I had the American sources brought to my office from the New York State Library so that I could work on them as time permitted. At the university I could devote myself full-time to pulling the threads together. In the summer of 1968 I combined Moore's research notes with my own and wrote the introduction to the work in my Keene Valley cottage without telephone or other distractions. George and Nina Winkel, our Keene Valley neighbors, both natives of Germany, dropped their own work to translate German sources for me.

Two of our Albany graduate students in anthropology produced the index. One day I walked by the room where the women were working and overheard a snatch of conversation. One said to the other, "I can't wait to see the book in print." The other replied, "I can wait for the movie."

The long delay of the project caused some concern in the Toronto office of the Champlain Society and became a source of derision later. The two volumes (Fenton and Moore 1974) were priced at thirty-five dollars each; the set fetched some four hundred dollars on the antiquarian book market in Toronto as of the millennium. The joke is now on the society. A baker's dozen of Iroquoianists joined the society to receive the volumes as they appeared and subsequently dropped out. The work has been widely cited and favorably reviewed. Most recently, in a widely acclaimed work in the captivity genre, John Demos, colonial historian at Yale, relied heavily on our Lafitau research in reconstructing the native culture at Caughnawaga during the eighteenth century.[1]

Iroquois Redux

A decade after the Philadelphia Congress of ICAES of 1956, Frolich "Fro" Rainey retired as director of the University Museum after a long tenure. In preparing for the festivities honoring him, Fro made one request: that Bill Fenton invite the same Iroquois Indians who had come to Philadelphia and taken part in the 1956 Congress. Accordingly, I called Howard Skye, who had led the first party, and he reassured me that he would assemble the same people, with one or two exceptions and a few additions. The original members still talked about their previous visit.

Olive was slated to accompany me, but our daughter, Betsey, needed relief from caring for illnesses of husband and children. Olive opted to substitute and send Betsey to Philadelphia in her stead. The noted archaeologist Mary Butler and her husband, Cliff Lewis, hosted us in their modern home in Media. Betsey had thrown a few things in a bag for the last-minute flight and needed a dress for the reception that evening. Mary proceeded to dress her for the occasion. The two women went shopping for a suitable dress, and Mary rounded up white kid gloves and slippers. Betsey looked smashing.

The reception was an early evening affair, while it was still daylight in early summer, held in the University Museum garden. At the appropriate hour the Lewises drove us into Philadelphia, picking up Ward Goodenough on the way. Ward had followed me at Yale graduate school, and we had much to talk about. My Iroquois friends, wearing feathers, were already in the garden when we entered. George Buck, our neighbor at Lower Cayuga on Six

Nations Reserve in the summer of 1940, joined Betsey and me and put one arm around my daughter. A society reporter, notebook in hand, rushed over to inquire how we knew each other. Before I could say anything, George declaimed, "When she was a little girl we took in this lady and raised her up to be one of us." If this fabrication out of the captivity genre appeared on the society page, we never saw it. I suspect someone wised her up.

Next day in the museum auditorium, Howard Skye performed his version of the Discovery Dance, exhibiting a talent that surprised me and pleased Betsey, who had had dance instruction.

On Saturday morning we went to Fro Rainey's for an early lunch, which afforded time for talk of Yale and the careers of fellow graduate-school contemporaries, the faculty then, and our own futures. The first summer my family and I lived in Defreestville, Fro had brought a horse named Freckles, an Appaloosa, for our children to ride. It pleased us to hear that Freckles was alive and kicking. He had thrown son John, who suffered a concussion. Olive and I were at the state fair in Syracuse when word reached us. Betsey had shown great presence of mind in getting John admitted to Albany Medical Hospital, where we arrived after a frenzied drive over parts of the unfinished New York State Thruway to learn that John was recovering and to hear the chief of staff compliment us on having a daughter of such maturity at such a young age.

Sunday dawned bright and hot. Cliff Lewis proposed that we go swimming. Leaving Mary to clear the breakfast dishes, we three drove some distance out the Main Line to the estate of the senior partner of the brokerage firm with which Cliff was associated. A long drive led to the mansion, the largest house in Greek revival style that I recall. Four Ionic columns reached above the second floor midway of ample flanking wings. Cliff drove around the back, where a second, identical portico faced down the lawn to the pool of ample size. Sitting by the pool after a swim, I looked back to the house and remarked to Betsey that all of this would take some getting used to. Betsey replied, "It would take me five minutes."

So much for a weekend on the Main Line.

Return to Fieldwork: The League

With Lafitau in print, I was eager to resume fieldwork on the legend of the Iroquois League and its ceremonial enactment in the Condolence Council, which I had left off in the 1940s after the death of my collaborator, Simeon Gibson. Simeon and I had translated the text of the legend that Simeon's father, John Arthur Gibson, had dictated to J. N. B. Hewitt at the close of the nineteenth century and part of that given to Alexander Goldenweiser in 1912. Now, Simeon's nephew Howard Skye volunteered to carry on the work and prepare me for the condolence ceremony that Hewitt had promised to the Gibson heirs, a promise I was eventually able to fulfill (Fenton 1998).

Floyd Lounsbury suggested a way in which Howard Skye and I could recover the Goldenweiser text and learn its content. With two tape recorders, I would read a section of the text to Howard in my best Onondaga and record it while Howard listened. He in turn would render as much of the text as he recalled in proper Onondaga, which I would record on the second tape, using the first tape to prompt him. We soon learned how much text Howard could absorb and repeat before we turned to translating. We quickly developed a routine. One day as I read, Howard laughed. "You sound like some old Onondaga."

Thus, beginning in February 1969, Howard and I conducted a series of sessions spread over two years. During a recess in our work, Howard looked at me and asked, "How old a man are you?" I was then just sixty. "I am sixty-nine," he said. "If we are to finish this Deganawida business, we had better get on with it, for no one else ever will." That prophecy was unfortunately true.

Howard went the long trail on March 3, 1971, of complications of diabetes (the curse of his people) and prostate cancer, both afflictions for which his considerable knowledge of Iroquois herbals proved ineffective. I kept in touch with his urologist, who assured me that Howard might resume work with me. During a remission of his affliction we resumed work in June 1970 in what proved a most productive session, after which I went off to Keene Valley in the Adirondacks to transcribe the results of our work so far. Over the summer, Howard picked up a respiratory infection that left him too weak to cope with his primary enemy, and by Christmas he was back in hospital. He never lost interest in our work. Word of his passing reached me in the night. The message read, "Howard left us all this morning 3/3/71." Duties at home and at the university prevented my attending the funeral, but I wrote Howard's obituary for the *American Anthropologist* (Fenton 1972).

James Skye, Howard's nephew, offered to help me with the work and carry it through to the end. Sixty-five of the original 525 pages of manuscript text remained untranslated. Jim, a Cayuga speaker, attended Onondaga Longhouse and understood and spoke modern Onondaga. I soon discovered that the older terms in the text baffled him, but Jim was pleasant to work with, and by this time I was eager to finish rather than look for another informant. My main interest in the text from the beginning ran to what light it shed on the internal structure and processes of the Iroquois League itself, which I could handle, rather than Onondaga linguistics.

Floyd Lounsbury, brilliant linguist that he was, urged me to prepare the Onondaga text for publication. I demurred: although I might have a reasonably good ear for spoken Iroquoian languages, structural linguistics was not my forte. I would be willing to make the text available to a scholar of his choice, together with my notes on its content. Floyd's student Hanni Woodbury, an Iroquoian linguist with an Onondaga specialization, completely reworked the text and brought it to publication, graciously acknowledging my contribution.[2]

My work on the Gibson versions of the League tradition recorded by Hewitt and Goldenweiser did not go to waste. In chapters 4 and 5 of my *The Great Law and the Longhouse* (1998), I traced the discovery of the League tradition as an evolving concern among Iroquoianists from L. H. Morgan and Horatio Hale to Hewitt, Goldenweiser, and myself, and I then concentrated on Chief Gibson's versions.

The Wampum Controversy of the 1960s and 1970s

A working scholar may find it difficult to avoid at least one controversy in the course of a career. Sooner or later he may be called upon to take issue with prevailing public sentiment on a question of public policy on which he has special knowledge and a vested responsibility. As assistant commissioner for the New York State Museum and Science Service—in effect, director of the State Museum—I was charged with the care and preservation of the state's natural history and Indian collections, particularly the New York State wampum collection, the treasure of the State Museum. As the collection's designated keeper, I took special interest in the belts' care and preservation and researched their history. My responsibility stemmed from the law dating from the belts' transfer from Onondaga chiefs to the state in 1898. The museum had held the belts for some seventy years and, in effect, ownership had passed to the state by the principle of adverse possession.

Feedback from the civil-rights movement reached the Onondagas, and they became vociferous in demanding the return of the wampum belts, which they construed as a loan and not a sale. In 1967 a commission of the New York State legislature charged with revising or eliminating laws more than fifty years old hit upon the wampum law and, having accomplished little else, offered it to the press as a case in point. Regardless of the commission's motive, it lent legitimacy to the Onondaga claim. When the legislature repealed the law regarding custodianship of the belts, the Onondagas' activity peaked.

The Council on the Arts, regarding the belts as objects of art, soon got involved in the act. It sent a staff member to Onondaga to help prepare a case for repatriating the belts and awarded contracts to a lawyer prominent in Indian claims cases to recommend actions the council might take on Iroquois cultural possessions. So matters stood when I departed for the university in January 1968.

I was happily ensconced as research professor of anthropology at the new University at Albany, doing my own work, guiding our first doctoral candidate, and teaching a seminar or two when Hugh Flick, my superior at the State Museum, and John Broughton, my successor, called on me to represent the museum at a hearing on the wampum issue in the executive chambers. I agreed. Had I been unwilling to appear on behalf of the museum, I would have avoided much unpleasantness later. I mistakenly thought that historical truth would prevail over the social movement of the time. Fortunately, I had put my research in writing, pleading the case for keeping the New York State wampum collection intact. I circulated it among knowledgeable colleagues and sent a copy of my findings to Governor Rockefeller. I also submitted the piece to the American Philosophical Society for publication in its *Proceedings* and ordered separates for distribution (Fenton 1971).

On the day appointed for the hearing early in 1970, I appeared in the executive chambers to confront Irving Powless and one other Onondaga chief, who were accompanied by their attorney, Omar Ghobashy (on contract with the Council on the Arts), and Vine Deloria Jr., Sioux critic, who qualified his presence by saying, "I am working with the Indians on this matter." I explained that although no longer director of the State Museum, I had expressed my concern to the regents and the governor for keeping important collections intact. I then outlined the case for keeping the wampum collection, one of the state's great cultural treasures, in Albany.

Months after the hearing, during the fortieth reunion of the Dartmouth class of 1930, my old classmate Rockefeller sought me out, my brief in hand, to tell me that he had read it, but despite my historical findings, it would not "wash" politically. Wherever he appeared publicly, someone asked, "When are you going to give the Indians their wampum?" Iroquois activists are skilled publicists. They won over a *New York Times* reporter, who interviewed me and whom I sent to them, with the result that an op-ed piece I wrote was rejected. Advocates for the return appeared at functions in Manhattan and in Westport, Connecticut, where influential people gathered. My name went up on the "scalp pole" at Onondaga, and Mohawk writers at Akwesasne (St. Regis) contributed some outrageous pieces attacking me in *Akwesasne Notes*.

One other thing. For some years I chaired the Committee on Anthropological Research in Museums for the American Anthropological Association (AAA). It sought to encourage younger colleagues to utilize collections for research and screened candidates for stipends financed by the Wenner-Gren Foundation. As chairman of the committee, I drafted a letter in its name disputing the Onondaga demand for the return of the wampum belts, which, widely circulated, raised the hackles of some less-informed colleagues. The then president of AAA fired the committee. Though no longer a committee of AAA, we continued our program of encouraging younger anthropologists to use museum collections in research, and Wenner-Gren continued to finance the program. Several of our alumni hold important posts in museums now.

Matters dragged on for another two decades. My successors as director of the State Museum were less interested than I in keeping the wampum collection intact for research and educational purposes in the new Cultural Center in the "South Mall." Someone found a document I had overlooked, which was construed as supporting the "loan" view of the matter, and the director at that time favored repatriation. By then I had retired at age seventy from the university, and my interests centered in research and writing. My work on the Iroquois League (Fenton 1998) carries a chapter on wampum that omits reference to the controversy but represents my view as an ethnohistorian on a subject that continues to fascinate me.

Twelve named belts making up the New York State wampum collection were repatriated to Onondaga with due ceremony at Albany on October 13, 1989, and a grand homecoming was held later. In the view of Oren Lyons, "Onondaga Faithkeeper," I savor the dubious distinction of having held up their repatriation for twenty years.

New Zealand, 1975

The 1970s were a decade of unrest on American campuses. Student militancy spread from Berkeley and the great state universities of the Midwest to lesser campuses such as Albany. Students demanded representation at all levels of university governance in the name of participatory democracy. They expected to vote on matters affecting faculty careers, from the departmental level up to the university-wide Committee on Promotion and Tenure. Besieged by such issues, President Louis Benezet appointed a committee representing the principal disciplines of the university, of which I represented the social and behavioral sciences. It included two undergraduates, male and female. They were very vocal at first, but they cooled down as they realized that the committee had work to do and that as members they were expected to share the burden. I undertook a canvass of policies and practices at campuses in upstate New York. To our amazement, my gratitude, and the student's dismay, Albany's policy and practices showed in a favorable light. The students lost interest as semester finals drew near.

President Benezet was pleased by the work of the committee. Our report went to the faculty senate, where it was referred to a committee for review, which amounted to "decent Christian burial."

In an unrelated move, my department advanced my nomination to the rank of distinguished professor. Approved at the university level, it was granted by the SUNY administration. President Benezet decided to mark the honor by having an invited lecturer evaluate my career, followed by a dinner for related faculty and their spouses. Professor Anthony Wallace of the University of Pennsylvania addressed an assembly of students that afternoon as I sat on the rostrum, and that evening guests filled the Patroon Room for a free meal on campus. From the head table, where Olive and I sat along with Millie Straub, a university councilor, Tony Wallace, and President Benezet, it was a very civilized affair. (You can't lose on such a deal.)

In the autumn of 1974 I was due for a sabbatical. In a conversation with Fred Eggan, a fellow trustee of the Museum of the American Indian–Heye Foundation, about the Red Power movement among American Indians, we shared hints that a similar movement was afoot among the Maoris of New Zealand. The Maoris offered interesting parallels and contrasts with American Indians, particularly the Iroquois, who like the Maoris asserted a separate identity in a plural society. Because I had long personal experience with the Iroquois and because studies of "boundary maintenance" were much to the fore in social anthropology at the time, I wanted to examine the Maori situation myself. Besides, having studied under the Maori anthropologist Peter Buck (Te Rangi Hiroa) at Yale, I wanted to visit his roots. Eggan encouraged me to apply, with his backing, for a Fulbright travel grant, which was awarded, in addition to National Geographic Society support for fieldwork.[3]

Meanwhile, I had come to know the anthropologist Peter Wilson through mutual friends. Peter, on leave from Otago University in Dunedin, New Zealand, had studied under Pete Murdock at Yale after my time. Peter assured me that his colleagues at Otago would welcome me, that he would seek quarters for my stay, and that the students would benefit from the presence of a visiting Boasian. He cautioned me, however, that excepting the odd Maori laborer, Maori communities were concentrated on the North Island. I did not then realize that the distance from Dunedin north to Wellington and the nearest Maori *pa* (settlement) by air resembled that from Albany to Chicago.

Arrangements for my absence went forward at the university and at home. At my urging, the department hired Jane Hanks, an independent scholar who had earned her PhD at Columbia under Ruth Benedict, to fill my post for the spring semester. On the home front, Betsey and John came through as always in crises. John attended to business affairs during my absence, and Betsey took Olive home to Hamden, Connecticut, where three lively teenagers kept her amused.

I flew to New Zealand via Fiji, after a stopover in Honolulu to visit the Bishop Museum. The flight terminated at Aukland on the North Island, where we went through customs and immigration on February 1, 1975. My credentials as a Fulbright scholar attracted more attention than my Orvis rod and tackle bag, to which the customs agents were quite accustomed. They asked how I was going to divide my time. I wondered.

Peter Wilson met my flight into Dunedin on the South Island and drove me to Knox College, on the north side of the University of Otago, where Peter had arranged for me to occupy the quarters of a resident fellow on leave to study in Britain. Dr. Somerville, the master, greeted us wearing shorts, standard dress for Kiwi men, showed us around, and took me home for tea.

Knox College was Edwardian and Presbyterian, both in its exterior and interior. My suite featured a veritable "Niagara whizzer" pull-chain toilet and a great tub dated 1907, both imported from England. The quarters were austere but adequate: writing desk, large double window looking onto the kitchen court and at night into the southern sky, free of air pollution at that latitude.

Although residence at Dunedin was less than strategic for field-work, there were advantages in being accredited to the University of Otago, which had a great tradition in medicine and the sciences. Because Knox College drew its residents from every corner of the two islands and from all ranks of New Zealand society, I found myself plugged into a network of relationships for understanding *pakeha*—European New Zealand—society and for contrasting life in my own university. I enjoyed the hospitality of Wilson, Somerville, and Professor Charles Higham, chairman of the anthropology faculty.

Among many other such occasions, on my first Sunday in the country the Wilsons took me to the beach on a bay north of Dunedin. There I met some of their friends and colleagues, saw my first Maoris roasting mussels taken from offshore rocks, and watched teams of lifeguards competing at launching and rescue. I walked the beach but did not swim, and managed to get sunburned. The friendly Maoris insisted we have some of the mussels they were roasting, which were delicious. Finally, we all dug for cockles and soon filled buckets with them; we took them home and steamed them with garlic and butter. I felt at home with the native academics and the local scene.

At the end of my first week as visiting fellow at Knox College, I wrote to Olive describing my activities:

> I am rested and settled. I get up and get my own breakfast in a kitchen (like that of Mrs. Bridges in *Upstairs Downstairs*) adjacent to the senior common room. When term starts next week, they will start serving in the great hall, and I shall sit with the master and faculty at the high table, as in British university colleges. The master, Dr. Somerville, is a cross between Mr. Bellamy and Hudson in the same serial. The cleaning maid, who comes in once a week, talks like Rose.
>
> Mornings I walk through the botanical gardens to the university, thence down Castle Street to my office in a former residence adjacent to the anthropology offices in another converted residence. (The homesick Scots who settled Dunedin aimed to replicate Edinburgh.)

In another letter to Olive, I remarked on the way the faculty whose homes I visited invariably listened to recordings of classical music played on a small record player. "This seems to be the great thing out here among intellectuals," I said, "to overcome isolation and between rare visits of great symphony orchestras and chamber groups. I find their musical sophistication remarkable. They know the classics as we rarely do."

I passed the first month in Dunedin reading the latest anthropological books and monographs on the Maoris, historical works on Maori displacement, biographies, and the poetry and social criticism of the young Maori writers. The beautiful prose of Witi Ihimaera and the poetry of Home Tuwhare conveyed the imagery of the old Maori chants, and the protest literature paralleled that of contemporary American Indian writers, notably Vine Deloria Jr. If anything, the Maori protest was subtler and less bitter.

Beyond the walls of the university library, the trout were sending out their siren call. A fishing guide put me in touch with a young Canadian couple, Cole Shervill, a graduate student at Otago in fisheries biology, and Cathy Yseppe, who served in the public library. They were packing just then to go camping up north in order to fish the Waitaki River. This proved a happy arrangement. Soon after seven on Saturday morning, a Volkswagen Beetle rolled to a stop in the kitchen court beneath my window. Rod tubes and wading staffs protruded from half-open windows. I gathered my gear and sleeping bag, wondering where I and it would fit in. Cole and Cathy rearranged things to free the front seat for me, and Cathy squeezed in among the gear that filled the backseat to above the windows. We soon headed north toward Christ Church.

During the drive north, glimpses into the background of my new friends emerged, as well as their views of New Zealand society. As a Canadian, Cole Shervill resented being taken for an American and was quick to point out deficiencies in Kiwi culture and society. His forebears had come out from England and settled near Edmonton, Alberta, soon after the province opened. Cathy's grandfather had been a later immigrant from the Ukraine who had made a fortune buying and selling cattle among ranchers. Cole got me out on the streams, and I enjoyed knowing this young couple.

The Waitaki River is a great brawling stream, descending from mountains south of Christ Church to braid in strands on reaching the flatlands before entering the sea. The braids afford easy wading if one keeps a watchful eye on water level, which depends on its being impounded for hydropower generation or released higher up. Cole situated me on a braid where the water was knee deep and tied on a nymph of his own creation before he and Cathy sought deeper current below. I looked down to spot a sizable trout resting not two feet from my boot. I released the nymph in the current to drift. As I sought to retrieve it, something heavy smashed it and headed for deeper current downstream. Line was going off the reel. The rod bent nearly 180 degrees as I tried to turn the fish. Finally I succeeded and slowly brought it to net. Cole and Cathy, having witnessed my struggle, rushed up to say, "We expected your rod to snap." The rod—probably built by Wes Jordan, once principal rod builder at the Orvis Company—held, and I had taken a creditable South Island brown trout of twenty-four inches, five pounds.

On February 19, I wrote to Olive:

> This week Dunedin is full of medical doctors, here to celebrate the "Centeenary" of the medical college. Many of them are old Knox boys and are staying in college. I was invited to dine with them. I sat with a nice couple named Mandeno (French Huguenot derivation), who invited me to visit Te Kuiti in the King Country of the North Island, where he is superintendent of the regional hospital. I loaned him a wool shirt and a parka to go sailing. Mrs.

Mandeno was horrified that I might be planning to live among Maoris in a *pa*.

Walking from Knox to 'Varsity' and my workroom on Cumberland Street, at the foot of the hill I passed through the well-kept botanical garden, which Dunedin proudly sustains. Young men and women gardeners tend the flowerbeds. Returning, I frequently paused to rest and watch.

Cole and Cathy phoned me on February 20 that they would call for me on Friday at six o'clock to go down south to the Mataura, famous for its big brown trout, where Dud Soper and Dave Male, my fishing friends from home, had fished. They had secured the loan of a fishing camp for the weekend on the Wakaia, a tributary. Locally called a "crib," the camp was built of corrugated metal and fitted out with bunks, a cast iron stove, and other amenities. All very snug and comfortable. I was glad I had brought a sleeping bag. Outdoorsmen (virtually all males) in New Zealand either camped out or had access to such a facility.

Leaving Cathy to the breakfast dishes, Cole and I walked downstream to an outcropping of black coal that created a sizable pool, beyond which a herd of cattle with a presiding bull ended safe exploration. With one eye on the bull, who had other priorities just then, I cast and brought to net two brown trout one after the other—eighteen and sixteen inches, respectively. Satisfied, I moved upstream to a pool that I had noted coming down. The pool was occupied by an apparition out of the nineteenth century. A tall, gaunt man of sixty years, shod in Wellington boots and wearing a long black frock coat, was dapping with a ten-foot cane rod to fish rising to small flies. He got out of the stream, reached down, picked up a small terrier that had announced my presence, and put the creature in a coat pocket, an act he repeated whenever he crossed the stream. Looking me over, he remarked, "Mon, you'll no catch fish with that wee stick!" I opened my creel to show the two trout, which he admitted were "fair fish." He invited me to try the pool, but I failed to match the hatch.

We walked the banks together, he in the lead, for he knew just where to ford without filling his Wellies. We found Cole and Cathy by a fire they had kindled bankside, where they welcomed us. Our new friend, who lived in a trailer parked above for the summer, proceeded to tell us about the Wakaia, which he had fished for years, and to amuse us with tricks he had taught his terrier. We learned later that our friend served as a citizen member of the local angling district.

Returning to Knox on Sunday evening, I offered trout to the master and to Stuart and Julie Park, who had entertained me. On Monday I bought domestic white wine, which was dry and very good, retrieved the trout from the Knox refrigerator, and carried them to their place, where we grilled them with onion rings dipped in milk. While the fish were cooking, we picked blackberries for a sweet. A delicious meal discharging a social debt, as I described it to Olive in a letter on February 26.

Having spent the month of February on the South Island, I decided that I had read enough books on Maori ethnography and had best move up to the North Island for talks and a look around. To go the traditional way by train and ferry, I retained a booking agent, who proved quite the operator: he booked me first class on the ferry and installed me in Wellington's luxury hotel, the Captain Cook, named for the famed navigator. I was scarcely prepared for such palatial quarters.

Mr. Cox of the Fulbright agency, who had made appointments for me, expressed shock at my location in the most expensive hotel in Wellington. Cox knew his way around the New Zealand bureaucracy, which was most helpful and productive, and as we walked between meetings, his apprehension faded. He helped me to get the most out of my fellowship. He even applauded my weekends of sleeping out and angling.

I requested a meeting with Professor Joan Metzge, whose book on the Maori I had read at Peter Wilson's recommendation as the single best work on the people. So I made my way to Victoria University's anthropology department, where Metzge greeted me and took me to lunch at the faculty club. She urged me to play up the fact that I was Peter Buck's student. At the museum in Wellington, another of his students put me in touch with a Maori relative of Buck's, whom I later met at New Plymouth. (This maneuver shielded Metzge and her sources and put me on my own as an ethnologist.) Back at the office, she phoned her key Maori source and made all the arrangements. Marjorie Rau expected me when I arrived.

Among the foreign students who had been attracted to Edward Sapir's seminar on culture and personality in 1933–34 and by

Buck's presence at Yale, the one I came to know best was Earnest Beaglehole, of a distinguished academic family in New Zealand. It was he who summoned my courage to attempt the "orals" for the PhD. At Yale he met Pearl, a student from Wisconsin, later his wife, whom he took home to New Zealand. They had four children, and I read that he had died several years before my visit.

I called Pearl while at the Captain Cook; she failed to connect me with Yale, but she came anyway for the adventure of lunch at such a "flash" address. We sat at a table with a view of the harbor, and as we talked she gradually placed me in her memories of New Haven. Near us at another table, four young men of Maori heritage were engaged in animated conversation. Pearl recognized one of them as Witi Ihimaera, a rising literary star and author of a recent national bestseller, which I had read while in Dunedin. Pearl rose and approached their table, saying how much she enjoyed his writing, which obviously pleased him. Cordial introductions followed. The name Beaglehole elicited respect.

After lunch Pearl took me to a chamber music concert at the university and afterward to meet her elder son, David, a professor of nuclear physics, who had just received a prestigious award for his work. He received us in his office and listened to my mission. He reminded me of my own son John.

On the last day of my Wellington visit, Cox invited my contacts to lunch, which meant that they were informed of my mission and would not be opposed to my presence in their several jurisdictions.

My first incursion to the North Island consumed a fortnight and two days, during which I stayed at New Plymouth with relatives of Sir Peter Buck, met an amusing character named "Tui" Fenton, of Maori descent, and encountered Maori hospitality. The New Zealand Museums Association meeting there coopted me, and with them I visited Sir Peter's *marae* (meeting house or sacred platform) at Erunui and his tomb at Okoki Pa, which, alas, had been ransacked by collectors of Maori memorabilia. In both places we were received by Maori people of great dignity. Because I had traveled the farthest, I was invited to speak on the *marae*. I made a few remarks and closed with the Seneca *adonwen*ʔ (personal chant) that I had learned when I was adopted into the Hawk Clan—a performance that pleased the Maoris present, who seemed glad to hear that American Indians had customs comparable to their own.

By then I was in the charge of Marjorie Rau, whom Professor Metzge had alerted and who took me into her home. She had married a Tongan, a man of great physical strength who worked on the local road crew but was subject to frequent heart episodes that demanded her immediate attention. At home he cultivated his native taro in a kitchen garden. The house was immaculate, and they made me feel comfortable.

In driving some 693 miles, I weathered torrential rain brought by Hurricane Allison, which turned roads a soupy mess often hub deep. I had never seen such rain. I stopped on the way to New Plymouth airport to meet Professor James Ritchie, the Beagleholes' son-in-law, at Waikato University. He and Joan Metzge at Wellington were then the two active Maori scholars. Ritchie invited me to join his class so that his students could hear and question someone from the Boas tradition.

Returning to Dunedin resembled coming home for the moment. Everyone from the master to the boys at Knox was anxious to hear about my trip and the hurricane up north and to welcome me back to the land of the dour Scots. That week Mr. Cox, head of Fulbright New Zealand, came down from Wellington to talk with Otago University officials, confirming my status as a fellow and acknowledging Knox College's hospitality.

Word of my presence at Otago spread to the history department. Professor emeritus of history William Parker Morrell, a specialist on eighteenth-century colonialism, came into my office to invite me to lunch at his club. He just then was interested in Sir William Johnson's conduct of the 1768 Fort Stanwix treaty with the Six Nations Iroquois, which later served as a model for British treaties with the Maori. He was writing a book on the subject. One always learns something from such contacts.

Before going north to Plymouth for two weeks of fieldwork, I addressed Peter Wilson's seminar on the history of American anthropology, a subject I had internalized from teaching and could talk about from memory. The students received it well enough to invite me to join them at the Captain Cook pub afterward for a jug or two of beer. I found the students hungry for ideas, and they knew little about academic life in America.

From Plymouth I flew back briefly to Dunedin, where, on Palm Sunday, Cole and Cathy spirited me off to a beach north of town to hunt for "African lobsters" (giant crayfish) in caves offshore.

The younger men put on wetsuits, strapped on air tanks, and, carrying bags, swam out to the caverns, while I walked the beach. After two hours, the hunters resurfaced with a great sack of the creatures ready for the boiling kettle over a driftwood fire that I had kindled. In ten minutes we feasted on crayfish and tubers that the women dug from the beach and baked in the ashes. Of such are the hardy pleasures of the Kiwis.

Mid-April found me back on the North Island at Waitara, engaged in fieldwork, mostly observation and several interviews, which I taped. My entrée as student of Sir Peter Buck rapidly established rapport with local residents, many of whom were his kin.

I wrote on April 9 from Waitara Meeting House during a session that Marj Rau was conducting on Maori crafts—plaiting flax mats and bags. Four women from Rotarua tutored a group of girls. As I wrote, Marj was explaining the symbolism of carved ancestor posts and painted rafters. I felt at home in the *marae* setting with its separate cookhouse and adjacent dining hall, as in a contemporary Iroquois Longhouse. I looked up as Marj Rau came by to ask about my visit with her aunt Emily Haupapa that morning. Aunt Emily, in her eighties, living alone, had received me and listened to my tale of Peter Buck at Yale: how we all learned to chant the Haka, and the great parties that he and his wife hosted for his students. Emily Haupapa claimed to be his fourth cousin (her mother's mother and his mother's mother were second cousins). He always stayed with them when at home. I taped an interview of some two hours, between interruptions from a sawmill nearby.

Emily opposed teaching the Maori language in the schools; it should be learned at home, she felt. At this point Emily was tiring—time for her "lay down."

The next Sunday I attended a *hangi*: I watched men building an earth oven for the local version of a cookout, but the traditional way of baking taro and other tubers. On this occasion the oven was fired for a group of *pakehas*.

Marj Rau, perhaps tired of my persistent questions, arranged a visit to the home of the headman of her political subdivision, a man who had known Peter Buck from childhood, who could tell me of his homecomings in later years. The visit also relieved Marj of being my sole source on Maori life. The headman received us at his farm, and while Marj joined his women relatives in preparing dinner, he took me on a tour of Maori prehistory and to the scene of Buck's reunions with men of his age. As we walked the beach where they raced horses, my host pointed to the high bluff above us, to a projecting crag that he said was the perch of Maori men, their backs to the sea, from the *pa* behind it—a free fall of 150 feet. He pointed offshore to a reef where Peter had joined them in gathering mussels, which they gulped raw between shots of whiskey. Of such were Te Rangi Hiroa's homecomings.

Returning to the house, we sat down to a full-course chicken dinner, after which the headman led me to his study. I noticed a display of Maori memorabilia—tiki, dried fern, dance fan—on the wall above a shelf of books on Maori history and culture. Each book had a slip of paper marking, I presumed, the place where he had left off reading. I remarked on this. He answered, "I read to where I find a mistake, and no further." I heeded the lesson.

I had met a man I could work with. The first field trip is a throwaway. I never returned.

EIGHT

Life after University

Having retired from the university in June 1979, at age seventy, I became distinguished professor emeritus, activated my pensions, and devoted my energy to research and the writing of four books, including this one. During my first year of retirement, the National Endowment for the Humanities awarded me a senior fellowship, which enabled me to canvass the treaty file at the Huntington Library toward an ethnohistory of the Iroquois Confederacy. While awaiting the outcome of these endeavors I wrote a draft of *The False Faces of the Iroquois* (Fenton 1987).

I also joined the Documentary History of the Iroquois Project at the Newberry Library because it afforded access to source materials that fitted my research plans. The project assembled a file on wampum, to which I contributed a memorandum on the Museum of the American Indian–Heye Foundation's wampum collection that I had prepared for the museum's trustees (I served two terms as a trustee myself, 1976–80 and 1982–89). Just then, the first inquiry about the wampum belts came to the museum from attorney Paul Williams, representing the life chiefs of the Confederacy at Six Nations.

The trustees scheduled a hearing for late winter 1986, when the chiefs and their attorney might present their case for the return of eleven wampum belts that George Heye had purchased through dealers in 1903. Olive, my wife of fifty years, was mortally ill just then, but she urged me to go down to New York City for the day, which I did. When I arrived at the offices of the museum's attorney, the chiefs were already seated at the long conference table. Before I entered the room, young lawyers on the case intercepted me to assure me that they were prepared to defend the museum whichever way the trustees decided—to retain or return the eleven belts. Because of his long experience in the House of Representatives, I had asked Barber Conable, an attorney and chair of the trustees, to conduct the meeting. I sat at Barber's elbow.

Word of my wife's illness had reached the chiefs.[1] The meeting had barely opened when Chief Peter Skye addressed a few kind words to me and reminded those present of my studies at Six Nations, which he hoped would incline me to support their claim.

The meeting got down to business, and we heard Paul Williams advance the chiefs' claim. At noon the chiefs went out for fast food while the trustees deliberated over sandwiches in the office. When the meeting reconvened, I faced Leon Shenandoah (Thadoda: ho?) and Oren Lyons (Faithkeeper) of Onondaga, New York, who had come as observers and did not contribute. Once that afternoon Oren mumbled something about "Good Mind"; he is not an Onondaga speaker.

The trustees soon voted to return the belts, but it took another two years for the museum lawyers to overcome the legal difficulties involved in deacccessioning artifacts from a public trust in New York State.

Finally the ceremony of repatriation went forward on May 8, 1988. In an article in *Ethnohistory* (Fenton 1989), I described it from the perspective of both participant and observer. In addition, Michael Foster, an Iroquoianist then of the Canadian Ethnological Service, observed the ceremony while directing a cameraman from European Film Promotion's affiliate in Toronto and wrote up his notes within a week.

My observations of these events and my role in them were enhanced by my knowledge of two cultural patterns, one spatial, and the other sequential, that guide Iroquois behavior in such situations; I knew pretty much what to expect. During tribal business, chiefs in council sit facing each other as moieties on two parallel benches, but since this was a confederate matter, I expected them to sit in a tripartite arrangement, as if all the nations were represented, even though the Oneida and Seneca chiefs were absent. The seating arrangement can be diagrammed as follows:

Onondaga

Oneida   Mohawk

(Fire)

Cayuga   Seneca

Guest Nation

The events of the repatriation ceremony followed the order customary for a chiefs' council:

1. Preliminaries: greeting guests
2. Tobacco invocation
3. Returning thanks from earth to sky
4. Issue of the moment: two cultures (two-row wampum belt)
5. Accommodation: reciprocal gifts
6. Speaker for guests (WNF)
7. Closing thanksgiving address
8. Terminal feast

With these two basic patterns of Iroquois ceremonialism in mind, one is prepared to cope with most situations in Iroquois life.

My studies of the Iroquois ritual of condolence, the traditional history of the League, and the mnemonic belts of wampum that document it soon led me to investigate the career of Horatio Emmons Hale (1817–96); contact his descendants at Clinton, Ontario; participate in marking his gravesite; and later sketch his career (Fenton 1990). Inasmuch as the *Dictionary of Canadian Biography* entails a trip to the library for most readers, Hale's decade of Iroquois fieldwork, 1867–77, remains little known. Together with a committee of chiefs and G. H. M. Johnson, a bilingual Mohawk chief, as interpreter, Hale researched the oral history of the Iroquois Confederacy, examined the wampum belts that documented it and, in a memorable meeting at Brantford in September 1871, had the belts, which were brought to the Grand River in 1784, photographed along with the chiefs "reading" them. He also commissioned an artist to make drawings of individual symbols for a projected grammar of wampum symbolism. Hale sent copies of the photographs to concerned scholars, including E. B. Tyler of Oxford University, to whom he reported on mapping the languages of interior northwestern America.[2] J. N. B. Hewitt left me a copy of one of these photographs, which I carried to and from the field for years while researching the Condolence Council. I used it as the frontispiece of the 1963 reprint of *The Iroquois Book of Rites* and sent it to the National Anthropological Archives in 2001.[3]

To the dismay of later scholars, Hale's manuscripts and field notes went up in smoke when a fire destroyed his Clinton, Ontario, study. A grammar of wampum symbolism remains to be done.

In 2000 Denis Foley drove me to London, Ontario, for the meeting of the American Society for Ethnohistory, sponsored by the University of Western Ontario, with Regna Darnell as hostess. I did not prepare a paper but was told to appear at the annual meeting. To my surprise, Ray DeMallie read a citation awarding me the John C. Ewers Award for *The Great Law and the Longhouse*, which had been published in 1998, as the best book of the year on the ethnohistory of an American tribe. The award was given by the Western Historical Association at its meeting in San Antonio, Texas, whence DeMallie had brought it, knowing I would be present.

Since I had been unable to attend services for Jim Skye, Denis and I stopped at Six Nations over the weekend returning, to pay respect to Jim's close relatives—his wife, daughter, and brother. Chief Peter Skye, present wampum keeper of the Confederacy, received us cordially at home in the center of Ohsweken. (We had met at the hearing in New York.) His wife was making cookies, which we were soon eating. I sat face to face with Peter. After courtesy greetings, Peter reached for my hand and thanked me once more for my role in returning the eleven belts. Chief Skye believes, as did his grandfathers when they commenced the struggle for their return early in the last century, that these belts were all that was left of their heritage in the League tradition.

Removal to Cooperstown, New York, on May 1, 2001, after forty-three years' residence in Slingerlands and the preceding four years in the Albany environs, marked a significant change in my lifestyle. I had been living alone, rattling around in eight rooms, upstairs to study and bed, downstairs for meals and errands. My generation of neighbors had either died off or moved elsewhere, although the new generation gave me a splendid going-away party. Contact with the university at Albany, which I had enjoyed since 1979, soon faded as I put seventy miles between us. Yet several of the PhDs whom I trained have kept in touch, not to mention other colleagues. Denis Foley in particular has kept me involved in Iroquois studies, visiting frequently, driving me to conferences, bringing ritual holders here—when I assumed the role of informant and they asked questions as we shared tape recordings of their predecessors, to ensure that they got it right. I have tried to avoid new projects.

Four relatives made the move possible and bearable. Daughter Betsey made innumerable trips from central New York to Albany to sell the house, engage movers, and attend to details; her husband, Mayo, packed my fishing gear and tools and unpacked a mountain of packing cases left by the movers in the Cooperstown garage. Son John's wife, Diane, drove my station wagon loaded with me and my fishing tackle to Cooperstown, and John followed in Diane's car for their return. For the preceding month Diane had devoted days to packing the contents of my Slingerlands study and labeling boxes.

The present house, which Betsey found, overlooks Lake Otsego and the village from the east. The property adheres to "Lakeland Shores," an involuntary association of residents dating from the 1960s, which affords access to a lakeside park, swimming, boat launch, docking, and canoe racks. Betsey and Mayo, having sold their Homer house, live on Lake Street across the lake. The New York State Historical Association at Fenimore House holds the Thaw Collection of Native American Art and maintains a small but adequate library that serves me well.

An appeal to the museum program for a student who might like to earn a few dollars brought Andy Marietta, a real treasure with many skills: computer literate since age eight, at home with tools, and knowledgeable about the town and its cultural resources. Andy set up my study, unpacked and shelved books, moved stuff to storage in the basement, and set up my computer center. He continues to respond to my gaffes.

An event in Iroquois studies, to which I have already alluded, also involved me in 2001. Denis Foley arranged for a delegation of Six Nations life chiefs, led by Peter Skye, to visit me in Cooperstown, seeking reassurance that their version of the condolence ceremony accorded with the versions I had recorded in the 1940s from their predecessors. In a transformation of roles, I as ethnologist became informant, and they asked the questions as we all listened to tapes of the originals from the Library of Congress.

The chiefs hosted a dinner for us that evening at the Hotel Otesaga, and next morning we viewed the Thaw Collection at Fenimore House. Not a bad record for my ninety-third year.

I launched my ninety-fourth year with my eleventh and final visit as a "reader" at the Huntington Library, going back to 1950. Daughter Betsey and her long-ago Pembroke roommate, Kari Scott Gunn, conspired to enable me to spend six weeks in San Marino during January–February 2002. Kari flew out and back with me and proved an expert at freeway driving, and Betsey came out midway to enable Kari to return to duty at the Boston Museum of Fine Arts. Kari's presence and her father's eminence among his former students at the Huntington brought me unexpected recognition there. I worked on these memoirs while my book *The Little Water Medicine Society of the Senecas* was in production at the University of Oklahoma Press. The book appeared in October 2002, and at Christmas that year I presented copies to my five grandchildren, three of whom were present. Two of my seven great-grandchildren, Grace and Angus, blew out the candles on the cake honoring my birthday ten days before.

Introduction

1. See "The Publications of William N. Fenton," herein, for bibliographic information on works cited.

2. Anthony F. C. Wallace, "The Career of William N. Fenton and the Development of Iroquoian Studies," in, *Extending the Rafters: Interdisciplinary Approaches to Iroquoian Studies*, edited by Michael K. Foster, Jack Campisi, and Marianne Mithun (Albany: State University of New York, 1984), 2. Wallace provides the best summary of Fenton's career, paying special attention to his contributions in ethnology and ethnohistory.

3. Voget's overview of Fenton's contributions is in "Anthropological Theory and Iroquois Ethnography: 1850 to 1970," in Foster, Campisi, and Mithun, *Extending the Rafters*, 343–57.

4. See James Axtell, "Ethnohistory: An Historian's Viewpoint," *Ethnohistory* 26 (1979):1–13.

5. Thomas S. Abler, "Upstream from Coldspring: William N. Fenton and the Investigation of Seneca Culture in Time" (paper presented at A Celebration in Honor of William N. Fenton, Cooperstown, NY, October 2003).

6. In our description of Bill's celebration, we have borrowed heavily and shamelessly from presentations made that day by several colleagues. They are Thomas S. Abler, Ernest Benedict, Wallace Chafe, Harold C. Conklin, Maxine Crouse Dowler, Michael K. Foster, and Anthony F. C. Wallace.

7. See Joy A. Bilharz, *The Allegany Senecas and the Kinzua Dam: Forced Relocation Through Two Generations* (Lincoln: University of Nebraska Press, 1998).

8. See Hanni Woodbury, *Concerning the League: the Iroquois Tradition as Dictated by John Arthur Gibson*. Algonquian and Iroquoian Linguistics. Memoir 9 (Winnipeg, 1992).

1. Upstaters in Suburbia and at Home

1. Carved wooden masks worn by members of the Society of Faces, a medicine society among the Iroquois.

2. "Outdoor Wisdom," [Review of] *The Boy Campers*, by William Hillcourt. *The Saturday Review of Literature* 8, 17 (1931): 282.

2. At Yale and among the Senecas

1. An account of my first fieldwork appeared as the article "Return to the Longhouse" (Fenton 1972) and was later reprinted as "He-Lost-a-Bet (Howanʔneyao)" (Fenton 2001). Excerpts from the latter edition, reprinted with permission, make up the following section.

2. The Seneca clan system comprises eight clans, divided equally into two moieties, or "sides," which are seated on opposite sides of a symbolic fire. The Bear, Wolf, Beaver, and Turtle clans make up one moiety, and the Deer, Snipe, Heron, and Hawk clans the other. A Seneca clan is an exogamous kin group that reckons descent, inheritance, and succession matrilineally. A clan holds a "bag" of personal names that it awards at birth, changes at puberty, and confers upon a person's acceding to an exalted status. Adoption is a clan function, rarely nationwide.

3. The following account is taken from my typed field notes, written soon after the event.

4. In 1948, Olive and our three children would be adopted by the Beaver clan during the Green Corn Festival. Mary John and Myrtie Crouse urged their mother, Phoebe Nephew, matron of the clan, to choose the names and make the presentation. Olive received the name meaning "watch out for her opinion."

3. From Teaching to the BAE

1. Jesse Cornplanter (1889–1957), resident intellectual at Tonawanda, grew up at Newtown on the Cattaraugus Reservation during the height of the Handsome Lake religion, of which his father, Edward, was the leading preacher. Jesse knew collectors for museums and developed a reputation as an illustrator of traditional Seneca activities in his boyhood (Fenton, "Aboriginally Yours," 1978).

2. The reference here is to Rueben Gold Thwaites, ed., *The Jesuit Relations and Allied Documents: Travels and Explorations of the Jesuit Missionaries in New France, 1610–1791*, 73 vols. (Cleveland: Burrows Brothers, 1896–1901).

3. Upon the death of a chief, his "antlers of office," a string of white wampum, are set aside until the clan matron chooses a successor, when they are "requickened" (installed on the candidate) at a Condolence Council.

4. See Woodbury, *Concerning the League*.

5. After I refused to abandon Iroquois studies for work in Latin America, as requested by Steward, we went our separate ways. Steward was my

neighbor in McLean, Virginia; his two boys Mike and Gary played with John and Betsey. He actively opposed my appointment as senior ethnologist. John Swanton, upon retirement, went to Stirling and supported my candidacy for the position. Stirling, without consulting Steward, had me reclassified in Swanton's title.

6. See James W. Herrick, *Iroquois Medical Botany*, edited and with a foreword by Dean R. Snow (Syracuse: Syracuse University Press, 1995).

4. The War and Postwar Years

1. Wilcomb E. Washburn, *The Cosmos Club of Washington: A Centennial History 1878–1978* (Washington, DC: The Cosmos Club, 1978), 205ff., 216.

2. Son Harry was born February 1941 and died one year later.

3. The National Academy of Sciences was created by the U.S. Congress after the Civil War as an independent agency to advise the federal government on matters of science and technology. After World War I, the National Research Council was added to impanel and administer its committees in the name of the academy.

4. I had met Felix through my daughter who knew his daughter at the Francis Scott Key Elementary School in Washington, NE. The Fentons and the Cohens shared suppers. One such evening I remonstrated to Felix about an anthill in his garden, which he preferred to leave intact as a model of organization a million years old.

5. The National Research Council

1. Anthony F.C. Wallace, "Tornado in Worcester: An Explanatory Study of Individual and Community Behavior in an Extreme Situation." Washington, D.C.: Committee on Disaster Studies, Study no. 3. NAS–NRC publication no. 392, 1956.

2. The ICAES was a congress that met every four years during peacetime but had been interrupted by World War II. Its governing body, or permanent council, composed of representatives of adhering countries, met during the congress year and in the second year afterward to review the theme of the next host country.

6. The New York State Museum

1. The feathered headdress worn by Iroquois men.

2. *Report of the Commissioner's Committee on Museum Resources, 1962.* New York State Museum and Science Service, Albany. 1962. 61 pp.

3. I had recently sat on a search committee to find a replacement for Father John M. Cooper at Catholic University of America, and Gusinde was our choice.

4. William N. Fenton. 1965. American Participation in the VIIth International Congress of Anthropological and Ethnological Sciences, Moscow 3–10, 1964. *American Anthropologist* 67: 771–3. 127th Annual Report . . .of the New York State Museum and Science Service for the year ended June 30, 1965: 1–4.

5. Without waiting for the proceedings of the congress to appear (1967), I submitted the piece to *Ethnology* 4, 3 (1965): 471–84.

7. Research Professorship at Albany

1. John Demos, *The Unredeemed Captive: A Family Story from Early America* (New York: Random House, 1994).

2. See Woodbury, *Concerning the League.*

3. Parts of the following description of my sabbatical in New Zealand are drawn from my report to the National Geographic Society (Fenton 1983) and published with permission.

8. Life after University

1. Olive died on April 5, 1986, the day after our fiftieth wedding anniversary.

2. I saw and examined the Tylor copies during a brief visit to the Pitt Rivers Museum 1952, when I was concerned with other things. See Elisabeth Tooker, "A Note on the Return of Eleven Wampum Belts to the Six Nations Iroquois Confederacy on Grand River, Canada," *Ethnohistory* 45, 2 (1998): figs. 2, 3.

3. Tooker, "A Note on the Return of Eleven Wampum Belts."

1931

"Outdoor Wisdom." [Review of] *The Boy Campers*, by William Hillcourt. *The Saturday Review of Literature* 8 (17): 282.

1935

(With Cephas D. Hill) "Reviving Indian Arts among the Senecas." *Indians at Work* 2 (21): 13–15.
"The Tonawanda Indian Community Library." *Indians at Work* 3 (5): 46–48.

1936

"Guide Posts on Tonawanda Reservation." *Indians at Work* 3 (10): 31–32.
"Some Social Customs of the Modern Senecas." *Social Welfare Bulletin* 7 (1–2):1 4–7. (Also in *Indians at Work* 3 [21]: 10–14; 4 [6]: 41–42.)
An Outline of Seneca Ceremonies at Coldspring Longhouse. Yale University Publications in Anthropology 9. New Haven, CT. (Reprinted: Human Relations Area Files Press, New Haven, CT, 1970.)

1937

"The Seneca Society of Faces." *Scientific Monthly* 44 (March): 215–38.

1940

"A Further Quest for Iroquois Medicines." In *Explorations and Field-work of the Smithsonian Institution in 1939*, 93–96. Washington, DC.
"Problems Arising from the Historic Northeastern Position of the Iroquois." In *Essays in Historical Anthropology of North America.* Smithsonian Miscellaneous Collections 100, 159–251. Washington, DC.
"An Herbarium from the Allegany Senecas." In *The Historic Annals of*

Southwestern New York, edited by William J. Doty et. al., 787–96. New York: Lewis Historical Publishing Company.

[Research Report]. In Fifty-sixth (1938–1939) *Bureau of American Ethnology, Annual Reports,* 5–6. Washington, DC.

1941

"Masked Medicine Societies of the Iroquois." *Annual Report of the Smithsonian Institution for 1940,* 397–429. Washington, DC.

"Iroquois Suicide: A Study in the Stability of a Culture Pattern." *Bulletin of the Bureau of American Ethnology* 128 (14): 80–137.

"Tonawanda Longhouse Ceremonies: Ninety Years after Lewis Henry Morgan." *Bulletin of the Bureau of American Ethnology* 128 (15): 140–65. Washington, DC.

"Museum and Field Studies of Iroquois Masks and Ritualism." *Explorations and Field-work of the Smithsonian Institution in 1940,* 95–100. Washington, DC.

[Research Report]. In Fifty-seventh (1939–1940) *Bureau of American Ethnology, Annual Reports,* 6–7. Washington, DC.

1942

"Contacts between Iroquois Herbalism and Colonial Medicine." *Annual Report of the Smithsonian Institution for 1941,* 503–26. Washington, DC.

"Fish Drives among the Cornplanter Senecas." *Pennsylvania Archaeologist* 12 (3): 48–52.

"Last Seneca Pigeon Hunts." *Warren County Pennsylvania Almanac, 1943,* 4–5, 38. Warren.

"Songs from the Iroquois Longhouse. Program Notes for an Album of American Indian Music from the Eastern Woodlands." *Smithsonian Institution Publication 3691.* Washington, DC.

(Recorder and Editor) "Songs from the Iroquois Longhouse." *Folk Music of the United States, Archive of Folk Song,* Album 6. Washington, DC: Library of Congress.

[Research Report]. In Fifty-eighth (1940–1941), *Bureau of American Ethnology, Annual Reports,* 7–8. Washington, DC.

1943

(With Merle H. Deardorff) "The Last Passenger Pigeon Hunts of the Cornplanter Senecas." *Journal of the Washington Academy of Sciences* 33 (10): 289–315.

[Research Report]. In Fifty-ninth (1941–1942) *Bureau of American Ethnology, Annual Reports,* 5–7. Washington, DC.

1944

(Editor) "The Requickening Address of the Iroquois Condolence Council,
J. N. B. Hewitt." *Journal of the Washington Academy of Sciences* 34 (3):
65–85.

"Samuel Crowell's Account of a Seneca Dog Sacrifice near Lower Ohio, in
1830: A Commentary." *Northwest Ohio Quarterly* 16 (34): 158–63.

[Research Report]. In Sixtieth (1942–1943) *Bureau of American Ethnology,
Annual Reports*, 5–6. Washington, DC.

[Obituary] "Simeon Gibson: Iroquois Informant, 1889–1943." *American
Anthropologist*, n.s., 46 (2): 231–34.

[Obituary] "Simeon Gibson (1889–1943), Informant in the Iroquois
Ritual of Condolence." *Cranbrook Institute of Science News Letter* 13
(6): 5–7.

1945

(With J. N. B. Hewitt) "Some Mnemonic Pictographs Relating to the
Iroquois Condolence Council." *Journal of the Washington Academy of
Sciences* 35 (10): 301–15.

"A Day on the Allegheny Ox-Bow." *The Living Wilderness* 10 (13): 1–8.

"Place Names and Related Activities of the Cornplanter Senecas, I: State
Line to Cornplanter Grant: Northern Approaches." *Pennsylvania
Archaeologist* 15 (1): 25–29.

"Place Names and Related Activities of the Cornplanter Senecas, II:
Cornplanter Grant: The Place Where Handsome Lake Rose to
Preach." *Pennsylvania Archaeologist* 15 (2): 42–50.

"Place Names and Related Activities of the Cornplanter Senecas, III:
Burnt House at Cornplanter Grant." *Pennsylvania Archaeologist* 15
(3): 88–96

"Place Names and Related Activities of the Cornplanter Senecas, IV:
Cornplanter Peak to Warren." *Pennsylvania Archaeologist* 15 (4):
108–18.

"Pennsylvania's Remaining Indian Settlement." *Pennsylvania Park News*
44 (October), 2 pp.

[Research Report]. In Sixty-first (1943–1944) *Bureau of American Ethnology,
Annual Reports*, 3–4. Washington, DC.

Reports on Area Studies in American Universities. (Six reports prepared
for the Ethnographic Board, Washington DC. Mimeographed.)

1946

"Integration of Geography and Anthropology in Army Area Study
Curricula." *Bulletin of the American Association of University Professors*
32 (4): 696–706.

"An Iroquois Condolence Council for Installing Cayuga Chiefs in 1945."
Journal of the Washington Academy of Sciences 36 (4): 110–27.

"Place Names and Related Activities of the Cornplanter Senecas, V: The
Path to Conewango." *Pennsylvania Archaeologist* 16 (2): 42–57.

[Obituary] "'Twi-yendagon' (Woodeater) Takes the Heavenly Path: On
the Death of Henry Redeye (1864?–1946), Speaker of the Coldspring
Seneca Longhouse." *American Indian* 3 (3): 11–15.

[Research Report]. In Sixty-second (1944–1945) *Bureau of American
Ethnology, Annual Reports*, 3–4. Washington, DC.

"The Six Nations of Canada." *Proceedings of the Royal Canadian Institute* 11
(Series IIIA): 27–28.

1947

"Anthropology during the War, VII: The Arab World." *American
Anthropologist*, n.s., 49 (2): 342–43.

"Iroquois Indian Folklore. In Folklore Research in North America. Reports
of the Committee on Research in Folklore 1945 and 1946." *Journal
of American Folklore* 60 (October–December): 383–97.

(With Martha Champion Huot) "Seneca Songs from Coldspring
Longhouse, by Chauncey Johnny John and Albert Jones" [Program
Notes]. *Library of Congress, Archives of American Folksong*, Album 17.
Washington, DC.

(Recorder and Editor) "Seneca Songs from Coldspring Longhouse,
by Chauncey Johnny John and Albert Jones." *Library of Congress,
Archives of American Folksong*, Album 17. Washington, DC: Library
of Congress.

"Area Studies in America Universities." The Commission on Implications
of Armed Services Educational Programs of the American Council
on Education. Washington, DC.

"Conference on Iroquois Research." *American Antiquity* 12 (3): 207.

[Research Report]. In Sixty-third (1945–1946) *Bureau of American Ethnology,
Annual Reports*, 4–5. Washington, DC.

1948

"The Present Status of Anthropology in Northeastern North America: A
Review Article." *American Anthropologist* 50 (3): 494–515.

"The Fourth Conference on Iroquois Research." *Science* 108: 611–12.
(Also in *American Antiquity* 14 (2): 159–60.)

"Letters to an Ethnologist's Children." *New York Folklore Quarterly* 4 (2):
109–20.

[Research Report]. In Sixty-fourth (1946–1947) *Bureau of American
Ethnology, Annual Reports*, 5–7. Washington, DC.

1949

(With Ernest S. Dodge) "An Elmbark Canoe in the Peabody Museum of Salem." *The American Neptune* 9 (3): 185–206.

(With the Seneca of Coldspring Longhouse) "Another Eagle Dance for Gahéhdagowa (F[rank] G. S[peck])." *Primitive Man* 22 (3–4): 60–64.

"Seth Newhouse's Traditional History and Constitution of the Iroquois Confederacy." *Proceedings of the American Philosophical Society* 93 (2): 141–58. Philadelphia.

"Collecting Materials for a Political History of the Six Nations." *Proceedings of the American Philosophical Society* 93 (3): 233–38. Philadelphia.

"Medicinal Plant Lore of the Iroquois." *The University of the State of New York, Bulletin to the Schools* 35 (7): 233–37.

"Racism as a Barrier to Research and Economic Development: Indians of the United States." In *Proceedings of the Second Inter-American Conference on Indian Life, Cuzco, Peru, October 10–20*, pp. 1–5. Mexico City: Instituto Indigenista Interamericano.

[Research Report]. In Sixty-fifth (1947–1948) *Bureau of American Ethnology, Annual Reports*, 3–4. Washington, DC.

Report on Grants. In *The American Philosophical Society Year Book 1948*, 155–57. Philadelphia.

1950

"The Roll Call of the Iroquois Chiefs: A Study of a Mnemonic Cane from the Six Nations Reserve." *Smithsonian Miscellaneous Collections* 111 (15): 1–73. Washington, DC.

[Obituary] "John Montgomery Cooper." *Journal of the Washington Academy of Sciences* 40 (2): 64.

"Second Progress Report: Political History of the Six Nations." In *The American Philosophical Society Year Book 1949*, 186–88. Philadelphia.

[Research Report]. In Sixty-sixth (1948–1949) *Bureau of American Ethnology, Annual Reports*, 3–4. Washington, DC.

1951

(Editor) *Symposium on Local Diversity in Iroquois Culture.* Bulletin of the Bureau of American Ethnology 149. Washington, DC.

"Introduction: The Concept of Locality and the Program of Iroquois Research." In *Symposium on Local Diversity in Iroquois Culture*, edited by William N. Fenton, 3–12. Bulletin of the Bureau of American Ethnology 149 (1). Washington, DC.

"Locality as a Basic Factor in the Development of Iroquois Social Structure." In *Symposium on Local Diversity Iroquois Culture*, edited by William N.

Fenton, 35–54. Bulletin of the Bureau of American Ethnology 149 (3). Washington, DC.

(With Gertrude P. Kurath) "The Feast of the Dead, or Ghost Dance, at Six Nations Reserve, Canada." In *Symposium on Local Diversity in Iroquois Culture*, edited by William N. Fenton, 143–65. Bulletin of the Bureau of American Ethnology 149 (7). Washington, DC.

"Iroquois Studies at the Mid-Century." *Proceedings of the American Philosophical Society* 95 (3): 296–310. Philadelphia.

"Seventh Conference on Iroquois Research." *Science* 114 (2970): 588–89.

[Research Report]. In Sixty-seventh (1949–1950) *Bureau of American Ethnology, Annual Reports*, 4. Washington, DC.

1952

"The Training of Historical Ethnologists in America." *American Anthropologist* 54 (3): 328–39.

"Research on National Disasters." News Report, National Academy of Sciences, National Research Council 2 (1): 3–5.

"Seventh Conference on Iroquois Research." *American Antiquity* 17: 292–294.

[Research Report]. In Sixty-eighth (1950–1951) *Bureau of American Ethnology, Annual Reports*, 4. Washington, DC.

1953

The Iroquois Eagle Dance: An Offshoot of the Calumet Dance, with an Analysis of the Iroquois Eagle Dance and Songs by Gertrude P. Kurath. Bulletin of the Bureau of American Ethnology 156. Washington, DC.

"Cultural Stability and Change in American Indian Societies." *Journal of the Royal Anthropological Institute of Great Britain and Ireland* 83 (2): 169–74.

"A Calendar of Manuscript Materials Relating to the History of the Six Nations or Iroquois Indians in Depositories Outside of Philadelphia, 1750–1850." *Proceedings of the American Philosophical Society* 97 (5): 578–95. Philadelphia.

[Research Report]. In Sixty-ninth (1951–1952) *Bureau of American Ethnology, Annual Reports*, 3–4. Washington, DC.

1954

"Anthropology." In *Britannica Book of the Year 1954*, 47–49. Chicago: Encyclopaedia Britannica.

"The Hyde de Neuville Portraits of New York Savages in 1807–1808." *New-York Historical Society Quarterly* 38 (2): 118–37.

1955

"Factionalism in American Indian Society." *Actes du IVe Congrès International des Sciences Anthropologiques et Ethnologiques* 2: 330–40. Vienna.

"Anthropology." In *Britannica Book of the Year 1955*, 108–10. Chicago: Encyclopaedia Britannica.

"The Maple and the Passenger Pigeon in Iroquois Indian Life." *The University of the State of New York, Bulletin to the Schools* 41 (March): 253–59.

"Ninth Conference on Iroquois Research." *New York State Archaeological Association Bulletin* 5: 2–3.

1956

"The Science of Anthropology and the Iroquois Indians." *New York State Archeological Association Bulletin* 6 (March): 10–14.

"Toward the Gradual Civilization of the Indian Natives: The Missionary and Linguistic Work of Asher Wright (1803–1875) Among the Senecas of Western New York." *Proceedings of the American Philosophical Society* 100 (6): 567–81. Philadelphia. (Also *Library Bulletin of the American Philosophical Society for 1956*.)

"A Request from Scientist to Farmers." *Rural New Yorker,* April 7, p. 280.

"Iroquois Research" (Ninth Conference on Iroquois Research). *Science* 123 (3185): 69.

"A Century of Natural History Research in Albany." *Times-Union* (Albany, NY) Centennial Edition, April 22.

"Some Questions of Classification, Typology, and Style Raised by Iroquois Masks." *Transactions of the New York Academy of Sciences,* 2nd ser., 18 (4): 347–57. New York.

1957

American Indian and White Relations to 1830: Needs and Opportunities for Study. Chapel Hill: University of North Carolina Press.

"Factionalism at Taos Pueblo, New Mexico." *Bulletin of the Bureau of American Ethnology* 164 (56): 297–344.

(Editor) "Seneca Indians by Asher Wright (1859)." *Ethnohistory* 4 (3): 302–21.

"Long-term Trends of Change among the Iroquois." In *Cultural Stability and Cultural Change,* edited by Verne F. Ray, 30–35. *Proceedings of the 1957 Annual Spring Meeting of the American Ethnological Society.* Seattle.

1958

[Research Report]. In 119th (July 1, 1956–June 30, 1957) Annual Report, Bulletin 370, *New York State Museum and Science Service, Annual Reports,* 7–12. Albany.

"Preface." In *Systems of Political Control*, edited by Verne F. Ray, *Proceedings of the 1958 Annual Spring Meeting of the American Ethnological Society*. Seattle.

1959

[Obituary] "John Reed Swanton (1873–1958)." *American Anthropologist* 61 (4): 663–68.

[Research Report]. In 120th (July 1, 1957–June 30, 1958) Annual Report, Bulletin 374, *New York State Museum and Science Service, Annual Reports*, 7–15. Albany.

1960

"The Museum and Anthropological Research." *Curator* 3 (4): 327–55.

"The Hiawatha Wampum Belt of the Iroquois League for Peace: A Symbol for the International Congress of Anthropology." In *Men and Cultures, Selected Papers of the Fifth International Congress of Anthropological and Ethnological Sciences*, edited by Anthony F. C. Wallace, 3–7. Philadelphia, September 1–9, 1956. Philadelphia: University of Pennsylvania Press.

[Research Report]. In 121st (July 1, 1958–June 30, 1959) Annual Report, Bulletin 381, *New York State Museum and Science Service, Annual Reports*, 7–13. Albany.

1961

(Editor with John Gulick) *Symposium on Cherokee and Iroquois Culture.* Bulletin of the Bureau of American Ethnology 180. Washington, DC.

(With John Gulick) "Foreword by the Editors." In *Symposium on Cherokee and Iroquois Culture*, edited by William N. Fenton and John Gulick, 3–8. Bulletin of the Bureau of American Ethnology 180 (1). Washington, DC.

"Iroquoian Culture History: A General Evaluation." In *Symposium on Cherokee and Iroquois Culture*, edited by William N. Fenton and John Gulick, 257–77. Bulletin of the Bureau of American Ethnology 180 (25). Washington, DC.

"Folklore (American Indian)." In *Encyclopaedia Britannica*, 441–42. vol. 9. Chicago: Encyclopaedia Britannica.

[Research Report]. In 122nd (July 1, 1959–June 30, 1960) Annual Report, Bulletin 385, *New York State Museum and Science Service*, 7–12. Albany.

[Comment on] "Method of Studying Ethnological Art," by Herta Haselberger. *Current Anthropology* 2 (4): 367.

1962

"Ethnohistory and Its Problems." *Ethnohistory* 9 (1): 1–23.

"This Island, the World on the Turtle's Back." *Journal of American Folklore* 75 (298): 283–300.

"Introduction: Lewis Henry Morgan (1818–1881), Pioneer Ethnologist." In *League of the Iroquois*, by Lewis Henry Morgan, v–xviii. New York: Corinth Books.

[Research Report]. In 123rd (July 1, 1960–June 30, 1961) Annual Report, Bulletin 387, *New York State Museum and Science Service, Annual Reports*, 1–21. Albany.

1963

"The Seneca Green Corn Ceremony." *The New York State Conservationist* 18 (October–November): 20–22, 27–28.

"Horatio Hale (1817–1896)." In *The Iroquois Book of Rites*, edited by Horatio Hale, vii–xvii. 2d ed. Toronto: University of Toronto Press. (Reprinted: 1965).

[Research Report]. In 124th (July 1, 1961–June 30, 1962) Annual Report, Bulletin 393, *New York State Museum and Science Service, Annual Reports*. 1–5. Albany.

1964

(With Stanley Diamond and William C. Sturtevant) "Memorandum Submitted to Subcommittees on Indian Affairs of the Senate and House of Representatives." *American Anthropologist* 66 (3) Pt. 1: 631–33.

[Research Report]. In 125th (July 1, 1962–June 30, 1963) Annual Report, Bulletin 395, *New York State Museum and Science Service, Annual Reports*. 1–4. Albany.

1965

"American Participation in the VIIth International Congress of Anthropological and Ethnological Sciences, Moscow, August 3–10, 1964." *American Anthropologist* 67 (3): 771–73.

(Editor) "Captain Hyde's Observations on the Five Nations of Indians at New Yorke, 1698." *American Scene Magazine*. Tulsa, Oklahoma: Gilcrease Institute of American History and Art.

(Editor) "The Journal of James Emlen Kept on a Trip to Canandaigua, New York, September 15 to October 30, 1794, to Attend a Treaty Between the United States and the Six Nations." *Ethnohistory* 12 (4): 279–342.

"The Iroquois Confederacy in the Twentieth Century: A Case Study of the Theory of Lewis H. Morgan in 'Ancient Society.'" *Ethnology* 4 (3): 251–65. (Reprinted: In *The Emergent Native Americans: A Reader in Culture Contact*, edited by Deward E. Walker, 471–84. Little, Boston, 1972.)

(With Donald Collier) "Problems of Ethnological Research in North American Museums." *Man* 65 (100): 111–12.

[Research Report]. In 126th (July 1, 1963–June 30, 1964) Annual Report, Bulletin 401, 1–7, *New York State Museum and Science Service, Annual Reports*, 7–12. Albany.

1966

"Field Work, Museum Studies, and Ethnohistorical Research." *Ethnohistory* 13 (1–2): 71–85.

(With Donald Collier) "Problems in Ethnological Research in North American Museums." *Museologist* 99: 12–16.

[Research Report]. In 127th (July 1, 1964–June 30, 1965) Annual Report, Bulletin 407, *New York State Museum and Science Service, Annual Reports*. 1–8. Albany.

1967

"La théorie de L. H. Morgan de périodisation de l'histoire de société primitive et l'ethnographie modem." *Actes du viie Congrès International des Sciences Anthropologiques et Ethnologiques*, 4:461–74. Moscow.

"History and Purposes of the Conference on Iroquois Research." In *Iroquois Culture, History and Prehistory: Proceedings of the 1965 Conference on Iroquois Research*, edited by Elisabeth Tooker, 3–4. Albany: New York State Museum and Science Service.

"From Longhouse to Ranch-type House: The Second Housing Revolution of the Seneca Nation." In *Iroquois Culture, History and Pre-history: Proceedings of the 1965 Conference on Iroquois Research*, edited by Elisabeth Tooker, 7–22. Albany: New York State Museum and Science Service.

[Research Report]. In 128th (July 1, 1965–June 30, 1966) Annual Report, Bulletin 409, *New York State Museum and Science Service, Annual Reports*. 1–6. Albany.

1968

(Editor) *Parker on the Iroquois*. Syracuse, NY: Syracuse University Press.

"Introduction." In *Parker on the Iroquois*, edited by William N. Fenton, 1–47. Syracuse, NY: Syracuse University Press.

[Obituary] "MacEdward Leach, 1892–1967." *Journal of American Folklore* 81 (320): 104–5.

1969

"Kondiaronk." In *Dictionary of Canadian Biography,* 320–23. vol. 2. David M. Hayne, gen. ed. Toronto: University of Toronto Press.

(Editor) "Answers to Governor Cass's Questions by Jacob Jameson, a Seneca (ca. 1821–1825)." *Ethnohistory* 16 (2): 113–39.

"Conference on Iroquois Research 1969: Iroquois Research after 25 Years." *Newsletter of the American Anthropological Association* 10 (10): 9.

"J. F. Lafitau (1681–1746), Precursor of Scientific Anthropology." *Southwestern Journal of Anthropology* 25 (2): 173–87.

"Anthropology and the University: An Inaugural Lecture." State University of New York, Albany.

1970

"A Further Note on Jacob Jameson's Answers to the Lewis Cass Questionnaire." *Ethnohistory* 17 (1–2): 91–92.

"The Funeral of Tadodáho: Onondaga of Today." *The Indian Historian* 3 (2): 43–47, 66.

1971

"The Iroquois in History." In *North American Indians in Historical Perspective,* edited by Eleanor B. Leacock and Nancy O. Lurie, 129–68. New York: Random House.

"Converse, Harriet Maxwell (1836–1903)." In *Notable American Women, 1607–1950: A Biographical Dictionary,* edited by Edward T. James, 375–77. vol. 1. Cambridge: Harvard University Press.

"Wright, Laura Maria Sheldon (1809–1886)." In *Notable American Women, 1607–1950: A Biographical Dictionary,* edited by Edward T. James, 680–81. vol. 3. Cambridge: Harvard University Press.

"The New York State Wampum Collection: The Case for the Integrity of Cultural Treasures." *Proceedings of the American Philosophical Society* 115 (6): 437–61. Philadelphia.

1972

"Iroquois Masks: A Living Tradition in the Northeast. In American Indian Art: Form and Tradition, 42–47." [Catalog of] An Exhibition Organized by the Walker Art Center, the Indian Art Association, and the Minneapolis Institute of Arts, October 22–December 31, 1972. Minneapolis.

"Return to the Longhouse." In *Crossing Cultural Boundaries: The Anthropological Experience,* edited by Solon T. Kimball and James B. Watson, 102–18. San Francisco: Chandler Publishing.

[Obituary] "Howard Sky, 1900–1971: Cayuga Faith-Keeper, Gentleman, and Interpreter of Iroquois Culture." *American Anthropologist* 74 (3): 758–62.

"Foreword." In *Cartier's Hochelaga and the Dawson Site*, by James F. Pendergast and Bruce G. Trigger, xiii–xxi. Montreal and London: McGill-Queen's University Press.

1973

"An Instructor's Librarian [Andy Peters]." Bulletin of the Friends of the Owen D. Young Library, St. Lawrence University 3 (2): 5–6.

"Ethnology and Ethnohistory as Tools for Interpreting the Past: The Case of the Iroquois." In *Clash of Cultures: The American Indian Student in Higher Education, a Report*, edited by Roy H. Sansdstrom, 111–16. St. Lawrence University, July 10–28, 1972. Canton, New York.

"Folklore (American Indian)." In *Encyclopaedia Britannica*, 520–22. vol. 9. Chicago: Encyclopaedia Britannica.

"B. B. Thatcher's Indian Biography (1832)." [Introduction to] *Indian Biography or, An Historical Account*, by B. B. Thatcher. vol. 1. Glorieta, New Mexico: The Rio Grande Press.

1974

(Editor and translator with Elizabeth L. Moore) *Customs of the American Indians Compared with the Customs of Primitive Times*, by Father Joseph François Lafitau. vol. 1. Toronto: The Champlain Society.

(With Elizabeth L. Moore) "Preface, Bibliographic Note, and Introduction." In *Customs of the American Indians Compared with the Customs of Primitive Times*, by Father Joseph François Lafitau, edited and translated by William N. Fenton and Elizabeth L. Moore, ix–cxix. vol. 1. Toronto: The Champlain Society.

"Lafitau, Joseph-François." In *Dictionary of Canadian Biography*, 334–38. vol. 3. Francess G. Halpenny, gen. ed. Toronto: University of Toronto Press.

"The Advancement of Material Culture Studies in Modern Anthropological Research." In *The Human Mirror: Material and Spatial Images of Man*, edited by Miles Richardson, 15–36. Baton Rouge: Louisiana State University Press.

1975

"The Lore of the Longhouse: Myth, Ritual and Red Power." *Anthropological Quarterly* 48 (3): 131–47.

1976

[Obituary] "Marian E. White (1921–1975)." *American Anthropologist* 78
(4): 891–92.

1977

(Editor and translator with Elizabeth L. Moore) *Customs of the American Indians Compared with the Customs of Primitive Times,* by Father Joseph François Lafitau. vol. 2. Toronto: The Champlain Society.

(With Elizabeth L. Moore) "Lafitau et la pensée ethnologique de son temps." *Etudes littéraires* 10 (1–2): 19–47.

1978

"'Aboriginally Yours,' Jesse J. Cornplanter, Hah-Yonh-Wonh-Ish, The Snipe, Seneca, 1889–1957." In *American Indian Intellectuals,* edited by Margot Liberty. 1976 Proceedings of the American Ethnological Society. Robert F. Spencer, gen. ed. St. Paul: West Publishing.

"Problems in the Authentication of the League of the Iroquois." In *Neighbors and Intruders: An Ethnohistorical Exploration of Hudson's River,* edited by Laurence M. Hauptman and Jack Campisi. Canada. National Museum of Man, Canadian Ethnology Service, Mercury Series Paper 39. Ottawa.

"Northern Iroquoian Culture Patterns." In *Handbook of North American Indians, vol. 15, Northeast,* edited by Bruce G. Trigger, 296–321. Washington, DC: Smithsonian Institution.

(With Elisabeth Tooker) "Mohawk." In *Handbook of North American Indians, vol. 15, Northeast,* edited by Bruce G. Trigger, 466–80. Washington, DC: Smithsonian Institution.

"Cherokee and Iroquois Connections Revisited." *Journal of Cherokee Studies* 3 (4): 239–49.

1979

"The Great Good Medicine." *New York State Journal of Medicine* 79 (10): 1603–9.

1980

"Gayë'göthwë:' Hadihadi:ya's Yi:'do:s" [Tobacco Burning Invocation, they cross the forest, the Yi:'do:s Ceremony]. In *Northern Iroquoian Texts,* edited by Wallace L. Chafe, 3–8. *International Journal of American Linguistics, Native American Texts Series 4,* edited by Marianne Mithun and Hanni Woodbury. Chicago: University of Chicago Press.

"Frederick Starr, Jesse Cornplanter and the Cornplanter Medal for Iroquois Research." *New York History* 61 (2): 187–99.

1981

"The Iroquois in the Grand Tradition of American Letters: The Works of Walter D. Edmonds, Carl Carmer, and Edmund Wilson." *American Indian Culture and Research Journal* 5 (4): 21–39.

1982

"John Canfield Ewers and the Great Tradition of Artists and Ethnologists of the West." In *Plains Indian Studies: A Collection of Essays in Honor of John C. Ewers and Waldo R. Wedel*, edited by Douglas H. Ubelaker and Herman J. Viola, 11–17. Smithsonian Contributions to Anthropology 30. Washington, DC.

1983

"Maori Acculturation." *Research Reports* 15: 213–20. National Geographic Society.

1984

[Obituary] "Johnson Jimmerson (1918–1984)." *OHIYONOH* 16 (November): 14–15. Allegany Reservation.
"Dan Brenan the Forgotten Master." *Rod & Reel* 6: 36–39.

1985

(Editor, with Francis Jennings, et al.) *The History and Culture of Iroquois Diplomacy*. Syracuse, NY: Syracuse University Press.
"Structure, Continuity, and Change in the Process of Iroquois Treaty Making." In *The History and Culture of Iroquois Diplomacy*, edited by Francis Jennings, William N. Fenton, et al., 3–16. Syracuse, NY: Syracuse University Press.
(Editor, with Francis Jennings, et al.) *Iroquois Indians: A Documentary History of the Diplomacy of the Six Nations and Their League*. Microfilm publication. Woodbridge, CT: Research Publications.

1986

"A Further Note on Iroquois Suicide." *Ethnohistory* 33: 448–457.
[Obituary] "In Memoriam: Harry Watt and Avery Jimmerson." *OHIYONOH* 26 (June): 4. Allegany Reservation.

"Leadership in the Northeastern Woodlands of North America." *American Indian Quarterly* 10: 21–45.

"Sapir as Museologist and Research Director, 1910–1925." In *New Perspectives in Language, Culture, and Personality*, edited by William Cowan, Michael K. Foster, and E. F. K. Koerner, 215–240. Amsterdam: John Benjamins.

1987

The False Faces of the Iroquois. Norman: University of Oklahoma Press. (With Charles T. Gehring and William A. Starna.) The Tawagonshi Treaty of 1613: The Final Chapter. *New York History:* 373–393.

1988

"Keeping the Promise: Return of the Wampum to Six Nations Iroquois Confederacy, Grand River." *Anthropology Newsletter,* October. American Anthropological Association.

[Biographical sketches] "Horatio Hale, Samuel Kirkland, Joseph-François Lafitau, L. H. Morgan, Asher Wright." In *Handbook of North American Indians, vol. 4, History of Indian-White Relations,* edited by Wilcomb E. Washburn, 648, 657–9, 670–1, 697–8. Washington, DC: Smithsonian Institution.

1989

"Return of Eleven Wampum Belts to the Six Nations Confederacy on Grand River, Canada." *Ethnohistory* 36: 392–410.

"Old Broken Nose." *Ethnohistory* 32: 408.

1990

"Horatio Emmons Hale." *Dictionary of Canadian Biography* 12: 400–403.

"Frank Speck's Anthropology." *Man in the Northeast* 40: 95–101.

1991

"Frank G. Speck's Anthropology (1881–1950)." In *The Life and Times of Frank G. Speck 1881–1950,* edited by Roy Blankenship. University of Pennsylvania Publications in Anthropology 4. Philadelphia.

1998

The Great Law and the Longhouse: A Political History of the Iroquois Confederacy. Norman: University of Oklahoma Press.

2001

"He-Lost-a-Bet (Howanʔneyao)." In *Strangers to Relatives: The Adoption and Naming of Anthropologists in Native North America,* edited by Sergei Kan, 81–98. Lincoln: University of Nebraska Press.

"Foreword." In *To Be Indian: The Life of Iroquois-Seneca Arthur Caswell Parker,* by Joy Porter, xiii–xiv. Norman: University of Oklahoma Press.

2002

The Little Water Society of the Senecas. Norman: University of Oklahoma Press.

In The Iroquoians and Their World

Nation Iroquoise: A Seventeenth-Century
Ethnography of the Iroquois
by José António Brandão

Your Fyre Shall Burn No More: Iroquois Policy
toward New France and Its Native Allies to 1701
By José António Brandão

Iroquois Journey: An Anthropologist Remembers
William N. Fenton
Edited and introduced by Jack Campisi
and William A. Starna

Oneida Lives: Long-Lost Voices of the Wisconsin Oneidas
Edited by Herbert S. Lewis
With the assistance of L. Gordon McLester III

Kahnawà:ke: Factionalism, Traditionalism,
and Nationalism in a Mohawk Community
By Gerald R. Reid

www.ingramcontent.com/pod-product-compliance
Lightning Source LLC
Chambersburg PA
CBHW031444280326
41927CB00037B/259